SMALL BUSINESS

B**I**G

PROFIT

WORK LESS, EARN MORE, BUILD WEALTH

JOSHUA KEEGAN

R^ethink

First published in Great Britain in 2024
by Rethink Press (www.rethinkpress.com)

The following names are the author's trademarks: Systems and Software, The Four Professionals, The Three Pillars, Bulletproof Business Model, Future Forecast, World Class Finance Function.

Disclaimer: The views expressed in this book do not constitute financial advice. The investment ideas discussed should never be used without first assessing your own financial situation and consulting a qualified financial adviser. Neither the author nor the publisher can be held responsible for any losses that may result from investments made after reading this book.

Contents

Preface

'If I had to live my life again, I'd make the same
mistakes, only sooner.'
—Tallulah Bankhead[1]

I admit it. I f*cked up.

In 2017, I was running a successful business that was
doing better than ever: we had doubled in size year
on year, we had a decent office and a team of people
in it, everybody knew our brand and our social media
pages were buzzing. On the face of it, we were smash-
ing it, and as the figurehead of the business, I was
getting all this praise at such a young age. Yet there

---

1   T Bankhead, *Tallulah: My Autobiography* (Harper and Brothers, 1952)

1

was a problem that no one else could know about: our finances were a mess, and we were losing money every month.

We were growing, but we also kept running out of money. Our solution was growth: get bigger and make more sales. Sales solve everything. Bring on a new client and use that money to pay off old expenses. As long as money kept coming through the door, we were sure it would all work out in the end.

Then we got caught out. I can't even describe the feeling I experienced. The realisation that I wasn't as smart as I'd thought and that our strategy to solve our financial issues was making them worse was crushing.

Three issues amounting to a six-figure financial black hole all came to the surface in a couple of weeks. We had unknowingly spent all our money on hold from our client account. Our accounting system had not been set up correctly, so all our sales were being overstated by the VAT amount and all our costs were being understated net of VAT. In layman's terms: we were making much less money than we thought. Finally, because of the second issue, we realised we had unknowingly accumulated a tremendous VAT bill to HMRC. Three simple mistakes, £100,000 black hole.

Did I mention that I'm a chartered accountant? I am the first to admit I should have known better. I was embarrassed to admit I had taken my eye off our finances, but even with my skillset, I wasn't able to live up to the demands of scaling an intense business and keeping on top of the numbers. If the bank balance was looking good, I just carried on. We were the biggest we had ever been, yet we were haemorrhaging money and had a huge financial obligation to our clients and HMRC.

Over a few weeks, I went from an optimistic, fun-loving entrepreneur to a highly stressed, anxious, sleep-deprived managing director of a failing business. What made the whole situation worse was that it was all my fault and could have been avoided. Failure was not an option, particularly with a team that was reliant on the business and a tremendous amount of our clients' money that had been lost. So, the recovery began.

The first port of call was financial clarity. I built a finance team so that numbers were always being produced by professionals no matter how busy I was, set up a reporting structure and set aside time to drill into my numbers every month. It was more painful knowing the financial picture at the start as it was so negative, but I knew having that knowledge was better than not.

Once I had clarity on where we were, I could work out where we wanted to get to and how we were going to get there. We created a business model and a financial plan which detailed exactly how we wanted the business to look financially and what we needed to do month by month to make it happen.

Around eighteen months later, we went from loss-making to generating a very healthy profit. To my surprise, this did not come from growth: we had made the business smaller and restructured the operations to generate much higher profits. The key learning for me here was that bigger is not necessarily better. You can often make more money with a smaller company that has far fewer operational headaches, team members to manage and clients to satisfy.

Over the following year, I continued to fine-tune the methodology for managing our business finances. I moved from playing the sales game to playing the profit game. If profit was going up, I didn't care if we got smaller or if sales were down. My monthly finance review was (and still is) the highlight of my month because I knew that the actions that came from it would be the highest value actions I could take as an entrepreneur. What I could not believe was that a focus on optimising the business for profitability not only meant we had a lucrative business, but that the business also required less input from me.

By 2020, the business was making over six figures in profit, but I was now focusing on other businesses and generating additional income in my spare time.

We received an offer for sale in 2021 that was too good to refuse. Upon exiting my first business for a life-changing sum of money, I was drawing £100,000 per year from my 'small' business. I was working, on average, 90 minutes a week (this made my hourly rate £1,282), which was a vast contrast to working 40 hours a week and still losing money just a few years prior.

Getting out of the black hole was a very lonely place. At the time, I believed that I was only one of a few entrepreneurs who'd underestimated the value of their finances and almost failed, but as I started speaking about this experience openly, I realised I was not alone, and that most entrepreneurs would be better off earning minimum wage than getting paid less to run a high-stress business. I now work with 100+ entrepreneurs every year and it is clear that the main driver of entrepreneurial poverty is a belief that growing your business will grow your bank account and make your life better. Once you reach a certain sweet spot, the exact opposite is true. Being a busy entrepreneur is not a badge of honour. Becoming overpaid and underworked is.

It's true. I did f*ck up and it was one of the most challenging experiences I've ever had as an entrepreneur. But it brought me to the knowledge I have today and to the Ultimate FD (Ultimate Finance Director) helping entrepreneurs learn from my mistakes and restructure their businesses for time and profit. As long as you want to improve your business, make more money, work less and build wealth, this book is for you.

Introduction

Ask an entrepreneur how their business is going, and they will normally answer with an update on how many sales they have made this month or how much they have grown. Most entrepreneurs obsess over the top line. They believe bigger is better – if the business is growing, then the bank balance will too.

Many entrepreneurs with big businesses are stressed and broke. They work 50-hour weeks managing a team or people that they don't necessarily like. They commute to an office which replicates the corporate life they were running away from. They may drink heavily at the weekend and dread the challenge of a chaotic hungover Monday. Generally, the bigger the business, the lower the margin, so most of these entrepreneurs are overworked and underpaid.

Bigger is not always better, and there is a new type of entrepreneur arising. One that simply needs a laptop and an internet connection to function. They have a low-cost global team that works when they sleep and communicates by WhatsApp. They have low over-heads and create highly lucrative businesses. They have a small business with big profits, and they have a lot more fun doing it.

It is these entrepreneurs who have both time and money. They have a business that fits their lifestyle. They are healthy and they work to live. They sleep well and eat well. Train in the mornings. Spend time with their kids. They do high-value work which they enjoy and get paid well for doing it. It is these entre-preneurs that are masters in keeping their businesses as small as they possibly can, while keeping their profits incredibly high.

Just because the infrastructure of the business is small, it doesn't mean that revenues can't be big or you can't be highly leveraged. We have seen entrepre-neurs achieve over £1,000,000 in annual sales, making £500,000 per year with a small team in a few hours per week. Small businesses come with smaller problems: small business levels of stress, the ability to provide high service levels, affordable systems, motivated teams and fewer management responsibilities. If you can overcome your ego, you can see that a small busi-ness is where it is at.

There is one challenge: to reap all the benefits of a small business and make good money, you need to work smart. Going out, making some noise and mindlessly growing the business is not strategic enough. You need to shift from playing the sales game to playing a profit game. You need to shift from the mindset of 'business-driven finances' to 'finance-driven business'.

Most entrepreneurs are so snowed under that their approach is to show up each day and do whatever the business requires of them. They meet the demands of their business no matter how obtuse or lavish the requests are. We need a bigger office. We need more team members. The sales team needs branded cars. We need a new management system. Everyone needs new laptops. The team needs pay rises. This supplier has put up their prices. This client needs a lower price or they'll leave. Sound familiar?

Every request reduces profitability, for which the typical entrepreneur's answer is growth. If you get bigger, you'll have more revenue and more profits. When growth results in more strain on the business, there are more of the same requests. The cycle repeats until you now own a large, chaotic business with little to minimal profit. This is an example of 'business-driven finances'. Your business has no incentive to make a profit – only you do. Your business is like a child. If I give a kid £10 and tell them to spend £5 at the sweet shop, I don't expect to see any change.

In contrast, a 'finance-driven business' has a clearly defined set of money-making rules, a clear growth strategy, a fixed set of budgets and a capacity plan. All of its decisions are made well in advance – the plan dictates the decisions. Profitable businesses are run by entrepreneurs who are willing to say no. They decide exactly what it will look like in a year, and it happens. No more disappointing years or curve balls meaning that you never quite get 'there' or meet your financial goals.

To operate a business with huge margins and minimal personal input, you need to be highly strategic and put finance at the forefront of your decision-making. There are three questions you need to be able to answer to have the roadmap to building your highly lucrative small business. It was these three questions that took me from a broke entrepreneur to a six-figure lifestyle entrepreneur doing work I love for a few hours a week:

- Question 1: Where are you now?

- Question 2: Where are you going?

- Question 3: How do you get there?

Each of these questions will form a section of the book. I will break down and give you the tools you need to figure each one out. By answering these three questions, you will naturally level up your business and grow to a level of confidence, clarity and money that you have never experienced before. Without further ado, let's dive in and I will share with you the unique, proven Ultimate FD methodology which has now taken hundreds of businesses from loss to profit.

You can find all resources mentioned throughout the book on my website here: www.ultimatefd.co.uk/small-business-big-profit/resources

PART ONE
WHERE ARE YOU NOW?

1
In Search Of Financial Clarity

L et's kick off with the story of Cat and Chris, owners of NW Living.[2]

NW LIVING

Cat and Chris knew that they wanted to quit their well-paid corporate jobs and had identified building a property portfolio as the vehicle to get them there. They got started by throwing everything they had at the task, working evenings and weekends on top of their demanding jobs to make the business work and grow aggressively. The first milestone they set themselves

---

2   J Keegan, 'Episode 54: From financial struggle to family time, with Chris McDermott', Ultimate FD podcast (26 February 2023), www. ultimatefd.co.uk/podcast-episodes/from-financial-struggle-to-family-time, accessed 25 July 2023

was £5,000 per month of income, as they knew this would allow Cat to quit her regular job and focus on the business full-time.

Fortunately, the corporate world had already installed in them the importance of knowing their numbers. Chris had set up an accounting system and was managing the accounts himself, but as the business got busy, he fell behind. This became a problem when the bank balance started to fall, payments started to bounce, and they couldn't understand why.

They believed they were at £2,500 per month profit, and with the deals they were doing, they should be hitting their £5,000 initial target within a few months. Cat was excited about finally quitting work; however, the bank balance reduction was alarming. The first step was to regain clarity was by establishing the answer to the question: Where are you now?

The answer was shocking. They had believed they were hitting £2,500 per month, but it was a lot less. Some of the properties were performing at much lower levels than expected and interest on the additional debts they had taken out had crippled cash flow.

Their problem was not the oversight on the debt payments or the poorly performing properties, but that they had relied on Chris to keep an eye on the numbers while working a full-time job and scaling a capital-intensive business. They had taken their eye off the ball and were haemorrhaging money. Now they had to regain control.

We implemented a new team to manage the accounts, restructured the way the accounts are produced, and diarised monthly reviews. In no time at all, Cat and Chris restored the performance of their existing portfolio and debt obligations. They ramped up the profitability on every property, and just a few years later, Cat has quit work and Chris is in the position to do so if he wants to. They now have two kids, pick and choose when they work, have additional business income streams and have well exceeded their initial financial goal.

 You can listen to Cat and Chris's story at: ultimatefd.co.uk/ podcast-episodes/from-financial-struggle-to-family-time

The first port of call

Financial clarity might not be exciting, but it is the foundation of every business. When you build a beautiful house, no one asks to see pictures of the foundations going in, but without them the house would not stand. If you want to build a high-margin business that performs like a well-oiled machine with minimal input, then the foundations are where you start.

A lot of entrepreneurs are painfully aware of the need to understand their numbers so they spend time reviewing out-of-date data, inaccurate reports and half-finished financial statements. This means that even the idea of reviewing the business finances is built up to be a high-effort task which yields minimal results and often it doesn't happen unless there is an emergency. Most resort to checking the bank balance for decision-making and using overly complicated spreadsheets for any kind of analysis. The risk here is huge.

17

According to a 2021 survey by CBInsights, the most common reason that companies fail is running out of cash.[3] This stems from low financial clarity. If you have total financial clarity at your fingertips, how can you run out of cash or manage your finances badly? But if you only have half the picture, your decision-making can only be half as good.

Here are some simple questions to help gain financial clarity when scaling a small business:

- Do you know what your profit was last month?

- Do you know what your net margin % was last month?

- Do you know what your gross margin % was last month?

- Do you have a formal finance review booked every month?

- Do you have a monthly balance sheet that you understand?

If the answer is no to any of the above, then you do not currently have the level of financial clarity you need. In this section, we are going to detail the system you can put in place to not only gain financial clarity right

---

3   CBInsights, "The Top 12 Reasons Startups Fail" (3 August 2021), www.cbinsights.com/research/report/startup-failure-reasons-top, accessed 12 October 2023

now, but how to set this up so you will always have all the financial information you need at your fingertips. What is even more exciting is that your input will be minimal once this is set up.

This is the first step in mastering your margins, making more money and releasing chunks of profit from your business that you didn't even know existed. Introducing the World Class Finance Function.

World Class Finance Function™ (WCFF)

I developed the World Class Finance Function (WCFF) in 2018 and since implementing it in my own businesses, the clarity it has provided has been pivotal to all the success I've enjoyed. It has allowed me to scale multiple businesses to six-figure profits, with the most recent getting there within a year. Using the WCFF allowed me to sell my first business for a record multiple, leading me to semi-retire and live off my multi-million-pound property portfolio at the tender age of thirty-three.

Not only has it been the key to my entrepreneurial success, but it has also helped me purchase and renovate my dream home, become the sole breadwinner and provide our family with ample holidays and incredible experiences. This system is what will give you an edge in the business world. While most entrepreneurs run around doing deals that don't make any money, you can sit back, cherry-pick your opportunities strategically and make a small fortune in half the time.

I have successfully implemented this system in over 100+ companies ranging from £30,000 to £5m of revenue and the principles always remain the same. But before we dive into the mechanics, let's be clear on what you can expect from a WCFF once implemented by going over the core principles.

World Class Finance Function™ characteristics

Generally, entrepreneurs fall into one of two camps: the ones who know how important rigorous financial management is, and the ones who have yet to learn how important rigorous financial management is. It's hard to help the entrepreneurs in the latter camp, because they must often first experience nearly losing it all or navigating a cash crisis (like I did) before they will act.

I'm assuming that you are reading this book because you do know how important financial management is, and you are not satisfied with how your business finances are currently being managed. Maybe you feel like your accountant just doesn't quite get the business. Maybe you believe you spend too much time pointing out seemingly basic mistakes made by your bookkeeper. Maybe you are doing the accounts yourself and are sick of constantly chasing your tail catching up during evenings and weekends. If any of the above sounds familiar, then a WCFF with the following characteristics is exactly what you need.

1. Real-time information only

Introducing the first WCFF rule: 'The 21-day turnaround'. There is little to no value in reviewing historical financial data (defined, for the purposes of this book, as anything over a month old). Most entrepreneurs live in a perpetual state of catching up with their finances and sporadically reviewing data that sheds light on a financial picture that has passed.

Businesses are fluid and dynamic, and financial information must be current to allow you to make good decisions based on the information you have today. The rule here is that all financial information should be produced for you to review within 21 days of the period passing. You should be reviewing last month's information within 21 days of the end of the month.

2. Commercial communication

Our next WCFF rule: 'You could explain it to anyone'. Most finance professionals speak a strange technical language called accounting. Accruals, pre-payments, manual journals, deferred tax, depreciation, amortisation, debtors, creditors, etc – the list goes on. Unfortunately, this is a second language which most entrepreneurs have never become acquainted with.

The problem is not that the entrepreneurs do not know it, but that accountants continue to use it when speaking to people with limited technical accounting knowledge.

A characteristic of a WCFF is that the finance professionals speak in commercial language. They explain why things are important and how this may impact commercial decision-making. The rule here is that you could explain the finances in your own language to anyone – whether a businessperson, family member or team member.

3. No blind spots allowed

Our next WCFF rule should be obvious but is often left unsolved: 'There must be an expert in every area'. Every business has its nuances and quirks when it comes to financial practices and requirements. A letting agency has client accounting, a building company has CIS payments, some companies are VAT registered, some have payroll and some don't. Unfortunately, there are very few accountants that can handle all of these specialist areas, but you do need a specialist in each of them, so don't skimp and leave a blind spot in your finances.

4. Unshakeable

This one is the key to feeling the freedom you're longing for – the WCFF rule: 'It still works when you are on holiday'. Finance functions that are managed by the entrepreneur are very rarely world-class. They may work occasionally, but when the entrepreneur gets busy (which is always) or goes on holiday, they quickly fall apart. You need a team of professionals to run the day-to-day financials for you so the numbers are up-to-date and accurate rain or shine. If it works while you are away on holiday, then you can classify this as World Class as it runs with minimal involvement from you.

5. Ad hoc analysis (without the delay)

The final WCFF rule: 'One working-day time limit'. Making smart, strategic and financially driven decisions as quickly as possible is arguably the most important role of any entrepreneur in any business. A WCFF should act as an enabler for that. For example, 'If we do this deal, how will it impact our profitability? Do we have enough cash to invest in this training course? What will happen if the interest rates on all our loans go up by 2%?'

You should be able to send a voice-note or email to your finance team in the morning asking for any kind of ad hoc analysis of your finances and receive a detailed analysis to allow you to make the right strategic decision by the end of that day. The rule here is comprehensive ad hoc financial analysis completed by a qualified professional within one working day of request.

Creating your own World Class Finance Function™

There are three steps you need to take to create a WCFF:

- Systems and Software™

- The Four Professionals™

- The Three Pillars™

Following these steps will fundamentally level up your business and work for businesses of any size. I am going to take you through each of these three elements in the next few chapters.

2
Systems and Software™

This is the first element of creating a World Class Finance Function. As Michael E Gerber says in his book *The E-Myth Revisited: Why Most Small Businesses Don't Work and What to Do About It*, 'The systems run the business, the people run the systems.'[4] Entrepreneurs that want to enjoy big business profits with the ease, low-stress and fun of a small business need to become systems experts. Systems are everything, and as James Clear so elegantly puts it in his book *Atomic Habits: An Easy and Proven Way to Build Good Habits and Break Bad Ones*, 'You do not rise to the level of your goals but fall to the level of your systems.'[5]

---

4   ME Gerber, *The E-Myth Revisited: Why Most Small Businesses Don't Work and What to Do About It* (HarperCollins, 1986)
5   J Clear, *Atomic Habits: An Easy and Proven Way to Build Good Habits and Break Bad Ones* (Random House Business, 2018)

This applies to setting up your WCFF and is the place to start.

Luckily for you, it has never been easier to systemise your entire accounting function, keeping costs down and value (and, therefore, profits) high. By the end of this section, you will know all of the systems you require and everything you need to do to get them set up. They can all be done in less than one hour at minimal cost, so there are no excuses whether your business is brand new or has been around for years – every entrepreneur needs the setup I am about to share. Head to the resources page to get a referral link and bonuses for signing up: www.ultimatefd. co.uk/small-business-big-profit/resources.

Action 1: Select your system

Choosing your accounting system is easy, because I am going to save you time and make the decision for you. Choose Xero. I have used over fifty accounting systems in my previous life as an accountant and continue to work with numerous clients who have a range of different financial systems. Nothing I have seen comes close to the seemingly simple, easy-on-the-eye accounting system which is Xero.

We recommend setting up Xero for every limited company you have, and if you have any self-employed income outside of drawings from your limited companies, then we recommend getting it set up for that too.

On rare occasions, we speak to entrepreneurs that are reluctant to part with the extra money (currently around £25 per month). These entrepreneurs are normally the ones that I referenced earlier in camp two – those who have not yet realised the importance of rigorous financial management. They do not see the value and almost always quote the annual cost to make it sound like a lot of money: '£300 per year for something I could do on a spreadsheet?'

In most cases, there is no helping or changing the mindset of such entrepreneurs, and if you are one of them, feel free to put this book down and pick it up again when you've realised the error of your ways. However, I'll share what I usually would to try and convince you. *Excluding* the potential extra money that you will save by knowing your numbers, just by looking at the system's features you will have:

- The ability to automate the sending of professional invoices and accepting payments

- Automatic payment reminders for chasing money due from clients

- A place to store receipts for your end-of-year tax submissions

- A way of recording any expenses due to you from the business

- An automated system for managing supplier payments

The list goes on, and this ignores all the value you will get from the financial clarity – which is the real prize.

Action 2: Complete the setup

Once you have selected your system, you need to set it up. The first port of call is to activate your bank feeds. These are connections that allow you to automatically download incoming and outgoing transactions from your bank account to your accounting software. For example, if you spend £10 on parking on your Santander Business account today, your bookkeeper can 'reconcile' this transaction tomorrow, which means this can be allocated to your profit and loss in real-time.

Make sure that all your bank accounts associated with the business are linked to Xero before you progress to the next stage but be sure to *keep your business and personal spending separate*. It is not required by law to have a separate bank account for each limited entity, but it is highly recommended. Wealthy entrepreneurs keep their business and personal finances separate for numerous reasons, but the phrase 'Don't sh*t where you eat' sums up the thought process behind this. Manage your personal finances however you like, but keeping your business account transactions to a minimum with minimal complications will improve the efficiency of your WCFF and make it far easier for any professional to run.

Action 3: Select your software

This is your final action. One of the handy attributes of Xero is their open API, which means that it can talk to other applications. For this book, we will call these applications 'software' and I would recommend two main platforms that will benefit you when connected to Xero:

1. Dext: If you're like me and you find hoarding a never-ending mound of receipts a massive pain, then you'll love Dext. This integration puts an end to saving receipts by allowing you to take a picture and email them to your accounting system (ie, Xero). Using scanner tech, the receipt is analysed and suggests the correct allocation for your accounts, so no manual input is needed.

2. MileIQ: Recording your mileage is crucial for taking advantage of your mile allowance at the end of your business tax year. MileIQ takes the hassle out of recording the date, purpose and miles of business journeys in your car. You can ditch the spreadsheets or notes on your phone as it automatically records mileage for you. You can even swipe right or left in the app to record whether the journey was business or personal. This integration automatically transfers the data to Xero and ensures you can claim your mileage.

Before you go off and start exploring new software, a word of warning on bespoke integrations. With Xero having over 1,000 integrations available, the possibilities for bespoke options are huge; there are HR tools that automatically add payslips to Xero or payment-taking systems that put the customer invoices directly into the system. It's worth exploring some of the options to see how you can further automate aspects of your business and free up your time.

However, most entrepreneurs make one of two mistakes: not trying to automate anything, or trying to automate everything. Neither camp is a good place to be, the first reason being that your time is finite. The second might feel less obvious, as automation is brilliant up to a point, but the downside is that the complexities they introduce eventually limit the entrepreneur's ability to step back and allow someone else to run the system.

Around three years into my first business, it was so well automated that you could simply tick off a part of a process checklist and, voila, task complete. This one action would trigger a bespoke email (based on previously inputted customer details) to be sent with a customised link for them to make a payment. Once the payment was received, the customer would be taken to a video to be shown the next steps and a form to fill out. So efficient. What's the problem with that? The problem is this was muddled together through lots of apps and workarounds. Over time, it prevented me from stepping away from the day-to-day business as I was the only one who understood how to fix it and change this setup. We had to simplify things to allow us to scale and for me to free myself. The sentiment here is to tread carefully. You need to size up the iceberg and decide if the juice is worth the squeeze.

There are three points to consider when contemplating a bespoke integration:

1. **Cost to benefit ratio:** Will this integration save time even when it's not working well? There can be massive benefits and efficiency savings by integrating systems, but ask yourself: are those benefits worth it when the system is not working well or it breaks? There will always be issues, but you need to decide whether the benefits outweigh these.

2. **Specialist requirements:** Do I need a specialist to manage this integration? Some integrations, for example, SumUp (a payment terminal app), work well and are simple to set up. No specialist is required. However, other more sophisticated integrations will require system-specific knowledge. If this is the case, return to Point 1.

3. **Tried and tested:** Is there anyone you know who has been successfully using this integration for years? Don't be the canary down the mine for new systems. Ask around to see if you have a friend or a friendly competitor who can give you honest feedback about how their setup works and if they can recommend it or not.

Any system that integrates with your accounting system has the potential to optimise or cannibalise your business, so ask these three questions before you decide to give a system the green light. The manual way is sometimes the best way, as long as it's not being done by you.

Systems and Software checklist™

Before moving on to the second element of the WCFF, take a moment to check what you already have and identify the elements that you still need to get set up for your Systems and Software from the checklist below:

- Xero subscription activated for each entity
- All business bank accounts live with bank feeds
- All personal direct debits/standing orders moved from business card to personal card
- Software setup and integrated – Dext
- Software setup and integrated – Mile IQ
- Bespoke integrations decided
- Bespoke integrations set up

You are now ready for the next step of the World Class Finance Function: The Four Professionals.

3

The Four Professionals™

The second element of creating a World Class Finance Function is probably one of the most exciting parts of the process, as it involves you stepping away from managing your financials and bringing in people who, over time, will care more about your finances than you do. There are four professionals that every business needs to run their WCFF for them. Before you throw this book at the wall and shout, *'I can't afford that!'*, please bear with me, because this is nowhere near as expensive as you may think. Generally, I recommend that every business allocates 2–6% of revenue to spend on its WCFF which, once set up, will pay for itself through increased profitability, better decision-making and higher margins.

The motto of this element can be best summed up as: 'Right person, right role, right price'. Let's take a look at Tsen and Chris' story to see why this is so important when setting up your 'Four Professionals'.

ADAERO PROPERTY[6]

Tsen Wharton and Chris Dornan, owners of Adaero Property, had already scaled a very successful set of property and training companies before I met them. The businesses were operating well and they were making good money, but something continued to bug Tsen: he was still having to do all of his finances himself. Numerous times per week, he would log on and update his spreadsheets for a few hours.

He knew it was not a good use of his time, but after trying to delegate the arduous task to multiple bookkeepers, tax accountants and chartered accountants, he was never able to find anyone that did a comprehensive job and delivered what he wanted.

Tsen reached out as he had heard me talking about The Four Professionals on a podcast; he said his eyes lit up while listening and the model made total sense. Within just a few months, he went from reconciling everything himself to simply reviewing the reports. This meant he was able to ditch his fifty-two-tab spreadsheet, stop doing any finance work himself

---

6   J Keegan, 'Episode 23: I have a spreadsheet for that, with Tsen Wharton', Ultimate FD podcast (10 July 2022), www.ultimatefd. co.uk/podcast-episodes/i-have-a-spreadsheet-for-that, accessed 25 July 2023

and only spend small amounts of time reviewing comprehensive financial information produced by his world-class team. He shifted his focus to multi-million-pound developments and worked with his finance team to increase the profitability of the business.

Not only has the idea of a monthly finance review gone from pain to pleasure in his head, but his business is also now in the best financial shape it has been for years and he and Chris are taking home more money while putting in fewer hours. They are now freed up to focus on a new passion, building a business training other property investors.

 You can listen to Tsen's story here: www.ultimatefd.co.uk/podcast-episodes/i-have-a-spreadsheet-for-that

---

Invest and delegate

Steve Jobs once said that the secret to his success was 'that we have gone to exceptional lengths to hire the best people in the world.'[7] To have a WCFF, you need a world-class team of qualified professionals that know and care about your business's finances as much as you do, speak in plain terms and do not require heavy management.

7   S Burns, 'Steve Jobs Talks About Managing People', New Trader U (no date), www.newtraderu.com/2023/03/24/steve-jobs-talks-about-managing-people, accessed 19 July 2023

Most entrepreneurs know they need someone to support them with their numbers, so they find a book-keeper or tax accountant to delegate this to. It all seems exciting at the start – they are often promised the world and are finally going to get some clarity on their finances and business performance. Unfortunately, it rarely works out. It's common that the support they enlist don't ever seem to get the numbers right, miss seemingly simple details, are late with the reports, or send through reports which make little sense.

This can lead to continuing to pay someone begrudg-ingly while being dissatisfied with the service or trying to find someone else and getting the same results. In some cases, entrepreneurs even revert to doing the books themselves, which leads us to a very important point. *Do not do this yourself. It is both above, and beneath, you.*

You cannot have a small business with big profits if you are a bottleneck. Your focus should be to only do high-value work and delegate anything that has a lower value. For example, if you want to make £100,000 per year from one business and work on that business for 25 hours a week, then your hourly rate (assuming 6 weeks a year holiday) would be equiva-lent to £86.95 per hour:

£100,000 / [25 hours × 46 working weeks] = £86.95

You should be looking to delegate any task that you can get someone else to do for less than this. I appreciate this is a mindset shift and a lot of entrepreneurs struggle with this in the early days, but hopefully you see that the principle is sound.

A top-notch, world-class qualified bookkeeper who will do most of the workload in your accounts will cost around £20 per hour, so by delegating all your bookkeeping you are making a £66.95 profit on every hour you spend doing something else productive. Your hourly rate right now may be lower than a bookkeeper's, but you are not going to get it higher by doing bookkeeping. You need to get out there and focus on generating profit for the business. This is why doing the accounts yourself is below you: it is well below your hourly rate and the value you can add to the business.

On the flip side, doing your own books is also above you. Xero is a gift and a curse. A gift in that you can have a world-class system at a small monthly price. A curse in that it makes it all look so easy that anybody can do it. You may be able to log in and start reconciling bank lines, and you may even enjoy it, but as your business evolves, transactions will naturally start to get a little more complex and it will not be long until you start to create a mess. If you do not know how to do balance sheet accounting, why you would raise a reversing journal, how to account for revaluation gains, depreciate assets and generate accrued loan interest, then you are out of your depth.

If you are still not convinced, remember that one of the main attributes of a WCFF is being 'unshakeable'. I guarantee that with the best will in the world, you will not always produce accurate reports on time no matter how hard you try as you will always be juggling urgent tasks in a busy business with important accounting tasks. Urgent will always win, and your finances will suffer as a result. So now, let's meet the professionals.

Professional 1: The Finance Assistant

Title: Finance Assistant

Focus: Operational finance

Qualifications: No formal qualifications required but experience preferred

Workload: High volume, low value

Workstyle: Urgent

Rate: £3–£15 per hour

The first professional is the Finance Assistant. They are the base of the triangle, providing the foundations for the whole system to function properly. The Finance Assistant does not require any formal accounting or bookkeeping qualifications, apart from a basic understanding of your accounting system and a strong eye for detail.

Their primary focus is what I call 'operational finance', which is the bookkeeping and finance duties required to make the business tick on a day-to-day basis. These duties would include credit control (chasing customers for payment), generating and sending invoices, adding receipts to the accounting system, processing Director expenses and making payments.

The common theme is that these are frequent tasks that have a customer or operations focus. For example, paying a supplier means that they can complete the work for the business. Sending an invoice to a customer is required for the business to start work for them. These are all tasks that can be delegated so that you can focus on higher-value activities.

The Finance Assistant is normally part-time, requiring only a few hours a day, even for large businesses. The role can also be filled by a Virtual Assistant (typically working overseas, which can be cost-effective) or an Executive Assistant.

In some cases where the workload is high, you may want to recruit a Finance Assistant solely for your business. For example, I hired a Finance Assistant to work 25 hours per week for a large trading business due to a requirement for rigorous credit control (tenants not paying their rent) and complexities around landlord statements and accounting. Both responsibilities are high-volume and customer-facing.

Moving on from a property business to where I am now with Ultimate FD, the demands of the business are different and the nature of the operational finance is minimal. This means that the tasks are covered by my Executive Assistant in 1–2 hours per week.

One key aspect of this role is time management, as the work is often urgent. These tasks need to be done in certain timeframes or they can cause major operational issues, for example, paying a supplier on time so that they start work on a major project and avoid causing additional costs.

Professional 2: The Bookkeeper

Title: Bookkeeper

Focus: Recs and checks

Qualifications: Technician (AAT or equivalent) or experience

Workload: Medium volume, medium value

Workstyle: Important, lower urgency

Rate: £15–£25 per hour

Bookkeeping is a well-known profession, but what does it mean? Many entrepreneurs think a bookkeeper is exactly what they need; however, they only make up a small cog in your financial team. The best way to get the most value out of your bookkeeper is to make sure you are using their time and skills correctly and for the right tasks.

In terms of qualifications, you want to look out for either a technician-style qualification like AAT in the UK (Association of Accounting Technicians) or enough years of experience that you can be confident they know what they are doing (be sure to check on references). In practice, I suggest a minimum of five years of bookkeeping experience at a similar type of firm to yours. This role has the potential to make or break the business, so a cheaper person with less experience won't save you money in the long run.

The focus here is 'recs and checks'. Recs means reconciliations, which is the allocation of one transaction to another. For example, if you spend £100 on lunch with your team and send the receipt through to Dext, the next day, your bookkeeper can log in to your accounting system and connect the bank transaction to the receipt and allocate it to an account.

You may have read that and be thinking, 'Well, yes, all that's obvious, so why do I need a bookkeeper? I could do that myself, or my finance assistant could.' You would be right, but while 80% of your transactions will be straightforward, it's the 20% that aren't that need the qualification. For instance, if you buy a laptop for work use, do you know how to capitalise it on the balance sheet and depreciate it on a fixed line basis annually? When you receive a loan from an investor where the interest is paid upon repayment, do you know how to accrue the interest on the P&L monthly? When one of your companies lends money to another, do you have the time to complete intercompany reconciliations monthly? When you pay your insurance for the year in advance, do you know how to allocate a prepayment over the following twelve months?

For most people without an accounting qualification, the answer to the above will be no. However, even if you do know how to do all this, remember our guiding principle: this is both above and beneath you for reasons shared earlier.

A vital characteristic of a WCFF is real-time information. Data becomes information when it is double-checked and accurate. It is your bookkeeper's role to perform these checks. A simple example of this is checking that your bank feed is accurate. We talked earlier about the value of bank feeds and the impact these have on creating a solid financial system, but what happens if one day, for whatever reason, a few transactions don't get brought over and it sends all your numbers sideways? It's the bookkeeper's role to get a physical copy of your bank statement every month and compare it with the imported one to spot errors like these.

A good bookkeeper will typically cost in the region of £15–£25 per hour. They complete medium-value work and have a medium volume of work, so they sit in the middle tier of the triangle between the Finance Manager and the Finance Assistant. They tend to work with both individuals closely. They complete important, less urgent work, which means the work is always required, but there is generally less time pressure about the work they need to complete. For example, if they get all bank lines reconciled by the finance review, they could work on these daily, weekly or fortnightly. However, while the timeframe is flexible, the importance of getting them done is high.

Professional 3: The Finance Manager

Title: Finance Manager

Focus: Reporting: data to information

Qualifications: Chartered Accountant (CGMA, ACCA, Other)

Workload: Low volume, high value

Workstyle: Important work only

Rate: £30–£60 per hour

Say hello to the missing link: the Finance Manager. This professional will add significant value to you and your business and build a bridge between you and the Bookkeeper. A world-class Finance Manager will also provide all the necessary insight to maximise your margin, increase your profitability and make profit-focused decisions.

As this role is of such strategic value, the Finance Manager needs to be a chartered accountant, a member of a registered body and have years of relevant experience. This means they will be qualified to advise your Bookkeeper, yourself, and your Finance Assistant on how they should complete their work in line with Financial Reporting Standards (basically the rule book on completing accounts).

The core focus of this position is reporting and analysing the data into actionable insights for you as the business leader. Their skillset is to help you understand the story that your numbers are portraying, allowing you to make commercial decisions. It is this person that should be able to speak your language, understand your needs as an entrepreneur and explain the accounts to you in such a way that you could then explain it easily to others.

If your sales are down but your profitability is up, they will help you understand exactly why that is. If you are concerned about what may happen to your profitability next year if some regulatory change comes in, they can work out the impact it's likely to have on you. Send them a voice-note for some ad hoc analysis today and receive it from them tomorrow.

Hopefully, you're starting to see the value they can add to your business, though there's a chance you may have seen the price tag above at £30–£60 per hour and thought, 'No way!' The good news is that with this setup, you're likely to only need them for a few hours a month. Remember: 'Right person, right role, right price'. This means that although they cost more than the previous professionals, they are working the least on your accounts, keeping costs low and value high.

Professional 4: The Tax Accountant

Title: Tax Accountant

Focus: Tax strategy and submissions

Qualifications: Tax specialist – ideally, industry specific

Workload: Low volume, medium/high value

Workstyle: End of the tax year

Rate: £800–£2,400 per year (£66–£200 pcm) depending on business complexity

This is the profession that most entrepreneurs are likely to already have in place, as annual tax returns are legally required and the fear of overpaying tax drives us to make this one of the first professionals we employ.

In most cases, our haste to get a tax accountant means we end up overpaying for an average service. One such example is a client of mine whose frustration came as they were paying high fees, but doing all the initiating and sending emails to the tax accountants telling them how their finances should be structured, when one expects it to be the other way around. This is commonplace, as generally, tax firms are based on scale, and the bigger they get, the better they do. However, this often leads to service issues. They also tend to charge more for every new company you have, as they can advise on some complicated structures and setups. This may be tax efficient, but it's an operational nightmare.

The good news is that when you employ the first three professionals and add a tax accountant on top, you make their lives simple, thus reducing their workload and the price, while increasing the value they will add as they can fill a more strategic role. Minimal work volume but maximum value is the aim of the game here, as they are responsible for two things: tax strategy and tax submissions.

Tax strategy is mainly concerned with efficient company structure, how to draw money tax efficiently and company-specific advice around more complicated tax matters. For example, is it better to sell my properties or sell the company shares with my properties in them?

Tax submissions are the submission of (normally) annual numbers to HMRC in the form of limited company accounts and self-assessments. They should review the numbers well in advance of submission and advise you on any additional tax efficiencies. Good tax advice could save you hundreds, if not thousands, of pounds, but an additional benefit of having their signoff is the backing of their professional indemnity policy. This means that if they get something wrong and admit fault and this costs you, they could potentially be liable for damages.

A huge benefit of a good tax accountant is that their advice gives you peace of mind and the confidence that you have done the right thing. Trust me, your business will get stressful at times, you do not want to be adding HMRC investigations and payment plans on top of that.

Cost-wise, the average tax accountant charges between £800 and £2,400 per year per limited company or other legal entity. You can expect additional fees for extra services like payroll or VAT submissions. Ideally, you should look for a responsive tax accountant who has a systemised business and is willing to negotiate on prices given all your accounts are updated and signed off every month by a chartered accountant (ie, the Finance Manager).

To summarise, this is what your financial setup should look like, with workload being high at the bottom of the pyramid and low at the top, but value being low at the bottom and high at the top:

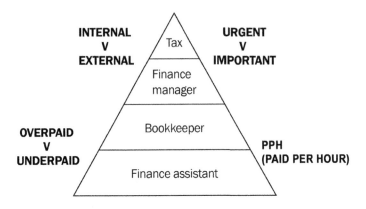

This is the dream team that will ensure that you have to do very little to manage your finances, so you can sit in a valuable strategic position with everyone else doing the heavy lifting. But, with great power comes great responsibility. Although your input into the monthly production of your finances is minimal, you still need to work relentlessly to improve them every single month.

Common mistakes

I wish I could tell you that just sharing this model at presentations or in this book will result in a seamless setup for your business, but there are several key, non-negotiable characteristics that you need to consider to get this working like a well-oiled machine. If you already have an underperforming team of finance professionals in your business, it is probably because you are making one, or all, of these mistakes:

Mistake 1: Misunderstanding the role of each professional

A common mistake is disregarding The Four Professionals model and going for three professionals. A Finance Assistant for low-value work, a tax accountant for tax advice and a bookkeeper or chartered accountant to cover both the Bookkeeper and Finance Manager role. Normally, one of two issues occurs here:

1. You find a qualified bookkeeper for £15–25 per hour and ask them to do both the bookkeeping role (recs and checks) and the Finance Manager role (reporting). The bookkeeper is underqualified to do financial reporting, so you get frustrated that they can never seem to deliver easy-to-understand, mistake-free reports. In this case, you are underpaying someone to do a job they are not qualified to do.

2. The other common issue is that you find a chartered accountant who is more expensive, say £30–£60 per hour, that is happy to do all your bookkeeping for you and is qualified to give you higher-level financial advice and reports. Sounds good on paper, but you are really paying someone far too much to do a job they are overqualified for. Commonly, this person takes on too much work and gets overwhelmed by bookkeeping for multiple clients. Once again, you end up with bad books and frustrations around their ability to provide accurate reports.

Pay a Bookkeeper a lower rate to do bookkeeping and a Finance Manager a higher rate to do financial management and you will not be disappointed. To try it any other way may save you money, but it is a false economy. Right person, right role, right price.

Mistake 2: Mixing urgent vs important tasks

If you mix urgent tasks like paying suppliers on time with important tasks like completing a bank account reconciliation, the urgent will always win and the important will never get done.

The mistake entrepreneurs often make here is combining the two lower-level roles: the Finance Assistant and the Bookkeeper. I made this mistake for years in my first business and always ended up chasing for financial information, only for it to be produced late and brimming with errors. At the time, I thought it was the person that was the problem, but every time I replaced them the same would happen.

It became apparent that it was the role. The urgent customer requests, payment runs and owner requests will always trump the quiet focused time required to do bookkeeping. To avoid this, don't mix urgent and important roles like the Finance Assistant and the Bookkeeper. There may be some financial savings here, but the solution will not last and the system will not be unshakeable, so it is ultimately a false economy.

Mistake 3: Keeping roles in-house

The Finance Assistant is generally the only role that I would recommend keeping 'in-house'. The working world is increasingly virtual, so 'in-house' could mean that they still work 3,000 miles away, but they are treated as a team member that you manage, invite to team meetings and are part of the company Whats-App group. The other roles should all be external and are services provided by external businesses with their expertise. There are three reasons for this:

1. Keeping these roles separate from the business means they don't get caught up in the noise of the business and can stay focused. Entrepreneurs can also be quite disruptive and that's not the energy we want in the finance function. Remember, a WCFF is designed to be unshakeable.

2. An external team allows you to delegate more and reduce your fraud risk. For example, delegating bank access so your Finance Assistant is more likely to pick up fraudulent activity quickly due to an unrelated team checking their work.

3. Let someone who has finance as their focus worry about the performance of your finance team. Let them hire and fire, control who works on your business and ensure that service levels

are world-class. You will have your hands full leading the company.

Mistake 4: Not being growth-proof

As your business grows and becomes more complex and you add in PAYE, VAT, CIS payments, client accounts, more limited companies, etc, the workload required to maintain your finances to a world-class level will increase. Your Four Professionals need to be able to grow with the business, so committing to hourly rates that can be scaled up and down as required is the best way to set this up.

In some of my companies, this entire solution has started as low as £75–£100 per month, but as the company grew, so did the hours, taking that monthly cost up to more like £300–£500 per month. As a percentage of revenue, the higher cost was lower. Small businesses with big profits tend to have low overheads by keeping a lot of their costs variable, based on usage.

The Four Professionals™ checklist

The Four Professionals are the game-changer you have been looking for. Once set up, your business will feel brand new, with fresh blood circulating in its veins. It is this team that will allow you to move away from being in the detail of accounts production to sitting at the top reviewing, directing and making profitable decisions. It is this single shift that allowed me to go from being a broke entrepreneur to making six-figure profits working 90 minutes a week. Before moving on to the final part of the WCFF, take a moment to identify elements of The Four Professionals you already have in place and identify the ones you still need to get set up:

- Set up a Finance Assistant
- Set up a Bookkeeper
- Set up a Finance Manager
- Contract a Tax Accountant
- Work through key mistakes to ensure they are being avoided

Now you have your team, you need to be clear on what you can expect from them, and the key monthly deliverables they need to produce, to allow you to maximise your value in the business and generate substantial profits. Every month, no matter what, you need The Three Pillars.

4
The Three Pillars™

This is the third and final element needed to create a WCFF. Financial statements are one of the most misunderstood and under-utilised tools in any entrepreneur's toolbox. Being fluent in finance is not optional (unless you want to be another busy and broke entrepreneur). You need to be able to read basic reports, understand them, and act based on what they are telling you. A pilot that doesn't understand the dials would make for a lousy pilot. The same is true for an entrepreneur. This does not require technical knowledge – just the ability to interpret, understand, and action.

By reviewing these powerful reports every month, you will make more money, draw more money, generate more wealth, build a business with a high exit value and make much better decisions. Are you scrutinising them every single month without fail? And if you are, are you achieving the benefits described above? The Three Pillars will provide you with all the necessary tools to manage the next conversation with your accountant.

Pillar 1: Profit and Loss (P&L)

Insight provided: Past performance

Profit and Loss (P&L) is typically the first report that a typical entrepreneur wants. Your P&L is a powerful decision-making tool when interpreted correctly. It summarises income and expenses during a specified period, so it tells the story of past performance, for example, how much money did the business bring in vs how much money went out? How did the business perform last month? What profit did we make? Did we make money or lose money?

You might wonder why we are interested in looking retrospectively if we are working in the present and looking towards the future. It's a good question and you may have heard the stock market disclaimer, 'Past performance is not indicative of future results.' This may be true for the stock market, but it's false in terms of company performance. By reviewing what has happened, you can make changes to what you are going to do. For example, if you made a loss last month because you overspent on taking the team out to the pub, then you can plan to reduce this next month. If an external cost rises, such as your tax accountant doubling their prices, you can find a more cost-effective tax accountant. Drawing insights and then *taking action* will impact your future company performance.

The five P&L components

The P&L is made up of five parts, starting with income at the top and net profit at the bottom. Different finance professionals use different terms to describe the same parts of the P&L, so I have listed the general terms below so you do not get caught out.

Component 1: Income

(Other terms: Sales, revenue, turnover)

Income is money received by the business in exchange for goods, services provided or income from investments.

In my first business, our income came from managing properties for landlords, finding tenants and completing maintenance work. Income is driven by the price of each of the products or services you sell and the quantity that you manage to sell.

Component 2: Cost of sales

(Other terms: Cost of Goods Sold (COGS), direct costs, variable costs)

This is the cost that you incur to produce the goods or services you have sold. These costs tend to vary with sales. If you sell more or less then you incur more or less costs, which is why they can be called variable costs.

In my case, our business cost of sales was made up of all the costs incurred to deliver on the income streams above. For example, once we had found a tenant, we needed to put them through tenant referencing, which we did using an external body at a cost to us. Likewise, when we completed a maintenance job, we also needed to pay the contractor for materials used. These are all examples of your cost of sales.

The rule here is that if you make a sale, then these costs go up. Likewise, if you have a bad month and make no sales, then you don't incur these costs.

Component 3: Gross profit

(Other terms: Sales profit, gross income)

Gross profit is the profitability of your product, service or investment. It's worked out by subtracting your cost of sales from your income:

Calculation: Income – cost of sales = gross profit

For example, say my letting agency generated an income of £500,000 last year and it cost us £150,000 to reference tenants, pay for maintenance labour and materials, etc. This leaves a gross profit of £350,000 (£500,000 – £150,000).

This is a good story, but it's not the full story. This figure tells us the profitability of our services, but not the overall profitability. To do this we need to subtract more costs, namely, our overheads.

Component 4: Overheads

(Other terms: Fixed costs, expenses, operating costs, operating expenses)

Overheads are the costs you incur to run the business and do not vary with the amount of income you generate.

If your income dropped to £0 tomorrow, what costs would you still have to pay for the foreseeable future? These are your overheads – the costs that your business incurs to run (as opposed to your cost of sales, which are the costs you incur to produce your products or services).

In my case, our overheads were extremely heavy, as it was a service-based business requiring lots of administrative, back-office support. We had a large payroll, plus subscriptions such as our accounting software and management systems, as well as an office lease. Regardless of how many sales we made, we still incurred these costs. They were fixed, which is why they were classed as overheads. When we deduct overheads from our gross profit, we get our net profit.

Component 5: Net profit

(Other terms: Bottom line, operating profit, earnings before interest, tax, depreciation, amortisation – EBITDA)

The net profit is what is left of your income after all costs are deducted. Referring to the previous example of my letting agency, which achieved a gross profit of £350,000, our costs to run the business totalled £200,000 annually.

This would leave us a net profit of £150,000 (£350,000 – £200,000), which meant that at the end of the year we should have been able to show £150,000 of hard-earned cash in our bank account.

Common misunderstandings

The P&L tends to be the statement that makes the most sense to the entrepreneurs we work with, as they understand that it is the report that tells them how much money they can get their hands on. However, there are a couple of common understandings that hold entrepreneurs back in fully understanding how to utilise a P&L effectively:

1. Cost of sales vs overheads

Rule: Cost of sales varies with sales. Overheads do not.

When determining whether a cost is a cost of sales or an overhead, all you need to do is determine whether the cost is only incurred because of an additional sale (cost of goods sold) or if it is incurred regardless of sales (overhead). This is an important understanding when we move on to business modelling.

2. Gross profit vs net profit

Rule: Gross profit is the profitability of your product/service, whereas net profit is the profitability of your business.

You could have two businesses with the same products selling at the same prices with the same cost of sales, but if one has an office full of employees in London and the other outsources all its overheads to the Philippines to make the most of cheaper labour, the profitability of the businesses will be vastly different.

Your P&L report is the first port of call. You need a comprehensive P&L every month and for every entity so that you can scrutinise last month's performance and take action to improve the next month's. Do this for a few months and you will see changes. Do this for a few years and your business, income and life will be transformed.

Pillar 2: The balance sheet

Insight provided: Present value

If the P&L is all about the past, then our next report is all about the present. Plenty of entrepreneurs have a go at implementing a P&L for their business, some successfully, some less so, but very few attempt the balance sheet. There seems to be a consistent misunderstanding of the value and importance of a balance sheet. The balance sheet provides a level of clarity and control that the P&L can't. Every business needs a clear, understandable balance sheet that tells you (the entrepreneur) a story when you look at it.

When reviewing your balance sheet, the question you're looking to answer is, 'What is the financial position of the business right now?' We'll kick things off with a basic, and hopefully relatable, example of what your personal balance sheet may look like.

Balance sheet example

You have £2,000 in the bank. You owe £500 to your brother for the family holiday, you have a credit card to repay at £1,000, and your friend owes you £700. Your personal balance sheet would look like this:

Cash in bank	£2,000
Money your friend owes you	£700
Total	**£2,700**
Minus your set of liabilities:	
Owed to brother	£500
Credit card	£1,000
Total	**£1,500**
Net asset value	**£1,200**

This means that if your friend pays you back, and you then pay off the money you owe to others, you'd be left with £1,200 cash in the bank. The calculation is:

Your total assets of £2,700 – your total liabilities of £1,500

This means that you're worth £1,200 – also known as your 'net asset value' and your current financial position.

Why is this important for you to know? Well, imagine that tomorrow, your partner asks if they can book a lovely weekend away. They find a luxurious hotel and the cost is going to be £1,500. It seems expensive, but you log into your bank and see that you have £2,000 sitting there. You remember that your friend will pay you back £700 soon, so you decide you can afford it. This is decision-making based on your bank balance. You spend the £1,500, your partner is happy and on the face of it, there's no problem. But, let's look at your new financial position:

Cash in bank	£500
Money your friend owes you	£700
Total	**£1,200**
Minus your set of liabilities:	
Owed to brother	£500
Credit card	£1,000
Total	**£1,500**
New net asset value	**–£300**

Although you still have £500 cash in the bank and your friend owes you money, your assets no longer cover your liabilities. This means that you're insolvent: you cannot pay your debts owed with the assets you have. In this instance, if your debts get called in but you can't get the money owed to you, it becomes a 'bad debt' and creates a stressful and financially sticky situation.

In the above example, logging in and checking online banking resulted in bad financial decisions being made on a bad set of data. Your bank balance only gives a snippet of the overall picture, but too many entrepreneurs use this (as well as how they are feeling that day) to run their financial decision-making process. *Should I buy a new laptop?* Log into banking expecting to see £3,000 in there but you forgot you were due another payment that came in, so you have £3,800. Yes, laptop time! *Should I get a new website done?* Log into banking expecting to see £3,800 in there, but see £1,900. Oh. No new website this month. *Should I recruit a virtual assistant?* Log into banking... And so on. The problem is that if you'd happened to log into banking a day earlier or later, the account balance could have told a very different story and led you to make a very different decision.

You might not realise it, but your bank balance is lying to you. Looking at your bank balance to determine how healthy your business is, is like using the scale weight to determine how healthy you are. If two people weighed themselves and were both 100kg, does this mean they are both equally healthy and should make the same life choices moving forward? Or could it be that one person is a foot shorter and has a high BMI, whereas the other who stands a foot taller is an athlete and maintains a high muscle mass? If you just review the weight on the scale, the information you receive is too simplistic to show the real picture, but with enough insight to broaden the story, you can be better informed to make decisions.

The balance sheet masterclass

The first step is being able to understand your balance sheet and the moving parts. The balance sheet is made up of four key elements: assets, liabilities, net asset value and equity. These may have sub-sections, but to aid simplicity, we will just focus on the main sections.

I'll go through each part of the balance sheet, as well as the typical language used:

Part 1 – Assets: Defined as anything that has a potential future economic (monetary, productivity, company value) benefit to the business. For example, cash in the bank, the value of property owned by the company, a new laptop, the money customers owe for work done, any loans you've made to other companies and stock you've purchased to be sold. Bringing it back to basics, looking at your assets will tell you some of the following:

- How much cash you have in each bank account

- How much money you are due from customers in the form of unpaid invoices

- How much money you are due back from any loans you have made

- How much the assets you own in the company are worth

Part 2 – Liabilities: Defined as anything that is a future economic obligation to the business. These are the opposite of assets in that they will result in 'outgoings' from the business at some point. For example, the money you owe in the form of debt, the value of mortgages on assets owned by the company, the money you owe to suppliers for services or the value outstanding on credit cards. Among other things, a glance at your liabilities will tell you:

- How much money you owe to other people / companies

- How much interest you have accrued and not yet paid on each of those loans

- The value of any credit cards you have with balances outstanding

- How much money you have been invoiced for from suppliers and not yet paid

- How much you owe in the form of mortgages on properties held in the business

- How much corporation tax you are due to pay on the next payment date

Part 3 – Net asset value: Defined as your total asset value less the value of your liabilities. This indicates the 'book value' of your business, meaning that in a theoretical world, if you set aside the intangible aspects of your business such as your reputation, brand, Google reviews, etc and sell your business based on the balance sheet, this is the value of the business. If your total assets are £1,000,000 and your total liabilities are £500,000, then your net asset value is £500,000 (aka your book value). This is the worst-case value of the business if things go wrong and you have to liquidate (sell all your assets and pay all your liabilities). Your net asset value answers these questions:

- If I sold my business today, how much is it worth in a worst-case scenario?

- Have I created more assets than I have accumulated liabilities?

Part 4 – Shareholder equity or equity: Defined as the value of the company's obligations to shareholders.[8] This is perhaps the least understood area on the balance sheet, but is also one of the most crucial. In simple terms, shareholder equity indicates how much value you have in the business, either in the form of money you have put in (in the form of share purchases) or profits the business has generated (ie, retained earnings). Shareholder equity will always equal the net asset value mentioned above. If it doesn't, then it is wrong (hence the name 'balance' sheet). A glance at your shareholder equity will tell you:

- How much money you have put into the business

- How much profit you have made on the P&L in previous months

- What can you draw in the form of dividends

- What have you already drawn in the form of dividends

- An indication of the company's value if sold today

---

8   'Shareholders' equity', BDC, www.bdc.ca/en/articles-tools/ entrepreneur-toolkit/templates-business-guides/glossary/ shareholders-equity, accessed 21 July 2023

Three key points to understand

To put it plainly, a balance sheet is a list of all the company's assets, liabilities and shareholder equity at a single point in time. Think of your balance sheet as a glorified bank account which allows you to check on your financial position at any given moment; it tells you exactly what your position is now, but also what you can expect in the form of future inflows (assets) and outflows (liabilities).

The problem is, for many people not trained in accountancy, reading a balance sheet is like picking up a book that is written in Spanish when your first language is English. As soon as your accountant starts saying terms like debtor, creditors, accruals, payables and pre-payments, it can understandably get a little confusing. So, let's drill it down to the three key points you need to understand.

Point 1: The balance sheet always balances

The accounting equation that ensures accounts are always accurate is:

$$\text{Assets} = \text{liabilities} + \text{equity}$$

Or to state another way, for those who like a bit of maths:

$$\text{Assets} - \text{liabilities} = \text{equity}$$

This equation is paramount in accounting and will always be adhered to due to the invention of double-entry bookkeeping in 1458. This means that for every transaction in the bank, there must be two transactions in the books.

For example, if there was a line in your bank statement of £10,000 for a loan you've received, the two transactions would be:

1. Debit (Increase) Cash (Assets) £10,000

2. Credit (Increase) Loans (Liabilities) £10,000

We have increased our assets by £10,000 and our liabilities by £10,000, so the equation balances. Modern accounting systems will not allow the equation to not balance, which removes the ability to make mistakes.

The beauty of The Four Professionals system is that you don't need to understand all the ins and outs of this process or know what all the lingo is. All you need to understand right now is that for every line on your bank statement, there must be two transactions or postings in your accounts.

My Grandad, who was an accountant for his entire career, used to revel in telling me how they had huge canvases, sharp pencils and massive rulers to allow them to meticulously craft a set of company accounts. Maybe accounting was more of an art form back then. Fortunately for you, using an accounting system automates dual-entry accounting so you can put your sharp pencils and rulers away!

Point 2: There's a symbiotic relationship between the P&L and the balance sheet

We talked previously about the profit and loss account. So, what if I told you that your balance sheet and your P&L were symbiotic?

When you build a level of profit and you leave it in your company, your company is worth more, so your P&L is just an account on your balance sheet that gets examined in more detail while also allowing you to drive company performance.

Say you made £50,000 in your business last year and you decided not to take any of that money. Where does it go? This money now sits in your shareholder equity, in an account known as Retained Earnings. This is a very important account, as the amount in Retained Earnings dictates how much money you can draw from your company in the form of dividends which, in some cases, may be a tax-efficient drawing strategy.

By building your P&L, you're also building your balance sheet. And by building your balance sheet, you're building your overall company value. And this translates to your future wealth. As entrepreneurs mature, they start to focus more heavily on the balance sheet than the P&L, as when performance is covered, they are more interested in creating value and wealth.

Point 3: Your accountant needs to be told to explain things in plain English

Accountants tend to lack the language and the softer communication skills to fully explain how accounts work for their clients. Ever get on a call desperate to understand something, you get it by the end of the call, but then wake up the next day and are drawing a blank again?

What's worse is that your understanding is not a priority for most tax accountants. Maybe your view is that you don't care, as long as your tax bill is reasonable, but my view is that understanding your company submissions is crucial. Ultimately, it's you that is responsible for them and it's your business that is affected.

Saying this, you may have tried to get an understanding of your balance sheet and failed – as I mentioned above, accountants often don't worry too much about your understanding. This leaves you with the experience of logging into your accounting system and being baffled by what you see there. Unfortunately, this is the case for most entrepreneurs, and it's normally caused by what the industry calls 'end-of-year adjustments'.

How do these work? At year end, you may agree to some changes to be made to align with your tax strategy. However, these adjustments can often slip through the net in your accounting system, leaving you with the problem of having an incorrect financial guide. This means that every decision you make based on these figures in the future may be jeopardised. On the flip side, sometimes your tax accountant will post what we call 'journals' to make those changes, but they rarely back them up, and often just do it in the quickest and easiest way possible, resulting in the creation of theoretical accounts on your balance sheet and other areas.

The sentiment here is that whenever your accountant does your accounts, you should be asking them to provide a breakdown of all the adjustments they've made and the reason behind each one, written in plain English so you can refer to these notes for years to come. This will at least allow your Finance Manager to unpick these if needed and make your balance sheet easier to understand.

While a balance sheet may sound overwhelming, with this report it's best to start now and perfect later, as it's easiest to understand when it's new, small and tame. Do not shy away from it – review the sheet thoroughly and seek to understand it as it grows and develops. Over time you will become fluent in balance sheet language and you will have a lightbulb moment when you want to know something about your business and realise that if you simply check your balance sheet you will get the answer.

Remember, this is where wealth is created, so if you want to generate a six-figure income and be wealthy for decades to come, this is where you need to shift your attention and focus.

Pillar 3: The cash flow forecast

Insight provided: Future problems

The third pillar is your cash flow forecast which, as you may have guessed, is a statement of projected cash inflows and outflows.

Cash tends to be elusive for most businesses. I remember desperately calling my dad after spending the entire day in a coffee shop trying to work out why we didn't have as much cash in the bank as we should have. It just didn't make sense. We were profitable – so where was the money? I clearly remember him telling me, 'Cash is just very tricky, Josh. If you work out how to track and predict it accurately, you let me know.' Thankfully, I did.

Running out of cash for a business is like a plane running out of runway before it has taken off. In some cases, you may have gained enough momentum to get away lightly, but in most cases, it will bring things to a full stop. There is nothing more stressful for an entrepreneur than managing a cash crisis:

sleepless nights, waking in cold sweats, high anxiety and fear are some of the symptoms (speaking from experience). However, there is one experience that is worse than running out of money. It's running out of money *unexpectedly*.

As an entrepreneur, you will always need to spend some of your time managing cash, but there is a big difference between reactive cash management and proactive cash management. Reactive cash management involves constantly moving money around from different bank accounts, putting money back in, paying using credit cards, taking on debt, and scrabbling around at the last minute to make things work. Reactive involves spotting cash problems months in advance and dealing with them calmly before they become emergencies.

Every business's cash flow can become entirely predictable. You could be solving next quarter's cash challenges right now. Further in the book, we are going to dive into the exact statement you need, how to create it and how to update it.

Three key principles of cash

To round up your fluency in finance and finish our Three Pillars section, there are the three key principles of cash you need to understand:

Principle 1: Your P&L is not the same as your bank account

One of the common mistakes by entrepreneurs is assuming that if their P&L shows a profit of £10,000 last month, the bank account will also show an additional £10,000. This is often not the case. While the P&L does drive cash, the report cannot be used to get a grip on cash, because most accounting is done on an accruals basis. This means that revenues and expenses are recognised when they are earned or incurred, regardless of when the actual cash transactions occur.

If you make a £10,000 sale today and incur £5,000 of costs to deliver that service, but your client only pays next month, you would still recognise the sale in this month in line with the expenses to show an accurate gross profit of £5,000. If you recognised it in line with the cash transactions, then you would have a loss of £5,000 this month and a profit of £10,000 next month, which would not represent an accurate picture of the business's financials.

Accrual accounting provides a more accurate picture of a company's financial health, but the only drawback is you can rarely look at your P&L to determine your cash balance. Eventually, what is stated on your P&L will become cash, but by that time other cash inflows and outflows may have occurred, so you will never get a grip on it. That is why you need to manage cash as a separate entity.

Principle 2: Prevent problems before they become emergencies

Your business will always have cash problems, whether that is because you have too much or, more commonly, too little. Growth will always exacerbate cash issues, and if you have a business with chunky inflows and outflows like a property business then you better get good at meticulous cash flow management.

The key to successful cash management is to get as far ahead of the game as possible. By being proactive instead of reactive, you can prevent problems before they become emergencies. You should be able to see cash issues at least six months ahead, although we advise twelve months for good measure. Don't bury your head in the sand or wait until the week before to find the £50,000 you need to plug a hole. Start taking action months in advance and get everything lined up in advance. A lucrative, leveraged lifestyle business with high margins is built on proactive planning, not reacting to emergencies.

Principle 3: Timing is everything

Assuming you have a financially sound business (more on this later), then cash is only ever a matter of timing. It will always come good in the end. The aim of the game is to ensure the end is never too far away by ensuring you do not over-leverage yourself or commit to projects with high levels of risk and low margins.

When managing cash issues, the first port of call is to delay outflows and speed up inflows. This action alone can have a profound impact on your cash balance and get you through the toughest months. Please note we are not talking about cost cutting here (that comes as part of your P&L actions), but of delaying cash leaving your bank account and speeding up cash coming into your bank account for costs and revenues already incurred.

Keeping your day-to-day bank balance healthy comes down to some very simple and easy practices:

- Ensure clients pay in advance or as close to the invoice day as possible.

- Set up auto-reminders for overdue invoices to prompt clients to pay.

- Offer discounted rates for large orders paid upfront.

- Ask for the longest possible payment terms from suppliers (this needs to be a win-win, otherwise you may cripple their cash).

- Always seek to pay in arrears as opposed to advance.

Good operational cash flow management also considers the commercial needs of your suppliers and customers, so you need to find a win-win for everybody. (We will go into more depth on advanced cash management and explain how to manage one-off capital expenditures effectively later in the book.)

Three Pillars™, one ecosystem

We have now looked at each of the Three Pillars individually, but they are all cogs of one ecosystem – interlinked and interrelated. This is important to understand, as entrepreneurs first need to know what actions to take to improve on each pillar, as well as how these actions cause a ripple effect in improving the others.

This lack of understanding is common and it can cripple businesses. For example, if you continue to grow with expensive debt that has interest repayable at the end of the term, your P&L and cash flow may look incredibly healthy, but all of this comes at the expense of a poor balance sheet. This is like owning a million-pound horse which is 100% leveraged by the bank, with a leased Maserati and countless items of jewellery on finance. It all looks good on the outside, but is set to implode.

Conversely, we have worked with entrepreneurs that have focused purely on the balance sheet for their entire careers and built substantial wealth and profit, but struggle to fill their car each month as they have sacrificed cash flow by continuously seeking to pay down debt.

Finding the balance is key. The diagram above shows you how each of the Three Pillars relate and feed into

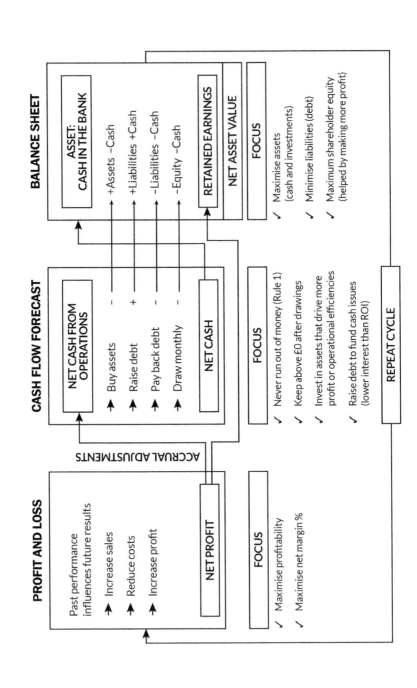

PROFIT AND LOSS

Past performance influences future results

↑ Increase sales
↑ Reduce costs
↑ Increase profit

NET PROFIT

FOCUS

✓ Maximise profitability
✓ Maximise net margin %

ACCRUAL ADJUSTMENTS

CASH FLOW FORECAST

NET CASH FROM OPERATIONS

↑ Buy assets   –
↑ Raise debt   +
↑ Pay back debt   –
↑ Draw monthly   –

NET CASH

FOCUS

✓ Never run out of money (Rule 1)
✓ Keep above £0 after drawings
✓ Invest in assets that drive more profit or operational efficiencies
✓ Raise debt to fund cash issues (lower interest than ROI)

BALANCE SHEET

ASSET: CASH IN THE BANK

+Assets –Cash
+Liabilities +Cash
–Liabilities –Cash
–Equity –Cash

RETAINED EARNINGS

NET ASSET VALUE

FOCUS

✓ Maximise assets (cash and investments)
✓ Minimise liabilities (debt)
✓ Maximum shareholder equity (helped by making more profit)

REPEAT CYCLE

one another, and what your focus should be for each one to build a small business with big profits.

The Three Pillars™ checklist

Once you have Systems & Software alongside your Four Professionals, the Three Pillars will be your focus. It may take some time to get to grips with the system and fully understand the meaning of each report, but over time you can become fluent in finance and operate at another level as an entrepreneur. Here's a handy checklist for the Three Pillars to assess what actions you need to take:

- Add a monthly meeting in the diary for a team monthly Finance Review. (Do not let the review end until you have fully understood all your numbers.)

- Complete your first P&L review.

- Complete your first balance sheet review.

- Create a set of actions from the review for clean-up work to make the accounts easier for you to understand.

- Identify operational actions to increase the performance of the business. These then need to be your focus for the month. Make the necessary changes to improve the numbers. Over time, dramatic improvements will occur!

Part One: Summary

The first part of this book has focused on gaining total financial clarity for where you are now. Implementing world-class systems and software, bringing on a qualified team of world-class professionals and becoming fluent in finance through your P&L, balance sheet and cash flow will fundamentally level you up as an entrepreneur. Most entrepreneurs spend their careers seeking to achieve what you have now achieved. It may have been uncomfortable, and you may have learned things you don't necessarily like about your financial position, but this is just the beginning.

Now the fun starts. Time to use this newfound financial literacy and understanding to take you on a journey to earn more than you could have ever imagined, while doing less than you thought was possible. On to our next question: where are you going?

PART TWO
WHERE ARE YOU GOING?

5
Know Your End Goal

Most entrepreneurs believe that if they watch motivational videos in the morning, take cold showers and commit to working every hour, then success in business is inevitable. If you want a more fulfilling, relaxed life with more income, then you need to get a little more strategic.

Before you build any business, you should be explicitly clear on what it will look like when it is finished. How big will it be? How much money will it make? How many team members? What prices will you charge? How much will you draw? How many hours will you work? If you leave any of these elements to chance, you will likely be continually disappointed. I'd like to tell you about a client of mine, Janice Minihan.

A PERSONAL PERSPECTIVE

Janice was a very organised entrepreneur. She had accounting systems and a team in place to manage her accounts. She was diligent in uploading receipts and making notes when it came to financial transactions. Getting a clear picture of Janice's businesses was not a problem, and they were doing OK, but she wasn't. She was exhausted. Burnt out, and by her own admission, 'Overworked, underpaid and spinning far too many plates.'

Over the years she'd continued to say yes to seemingly good opportunities and so she was now managing multiple companies: a letting agency, a deal sourcing business, a training and mentorship programme and a refurbishment management business. On top of this, she was building her own portfolio. Janice continued to jump feet first into these opportunities, but never fully knew where they were leading to.

At first, this can seem exciting, but after years of working 50-hour weeks, supporting a young family and still not being able to take much cash out of the businesses, this excitement starts to wear off. She knew that something needed to give.

The first question for Janice was: *'Where are you going?'* Initially, the answer was about the exciting plans she had to grow the business, get more clients and put her team in an office. I then reframed the question to, *'Where are you going personally?'* This question often results in a pause and a little more thought. To support her thought process, I elaborated: *'How much do you want to earn personally in the next twelve months?*

*What major changes do you want to see in your life? How
many hours do you want to work a week?'*

When meeting at a later date, Janice confirmed that
she wanted to work less – closer to 30 hours a week.
She also wanted to take home around double what she
was currently taking every month, so her family were
comfortable. Finally, she confirmed that she wanted
to move back to Australia and run the businesses from
abroad. These were things she'd always wanted. She
thought that if she kept working hard and showing up it
would all eventually just happen, yet year after year she
was disappointed.

It didn't take long for us to map out all the businesses
and understand why Janice was working too much
and not getting paid. In one, she was charging too
little, meaning every new client was not only time-
consuming, but also unprofitable. In some, she was
doing too much low-value work which her team needed
to pick up. In another, she had underperforming assets
which she needed to improve or sell. In some cases,
she had business partners under a deal that was no
longer serving her as it meant she only got a third of the
profits but had to do all the work. In just a few weeks
we had a simple plan that involved the need for very
little growth and no new clients – just a restructure
of what she had already built. We got explicitly clear
on where she wanted to be and then remodelled the
businesses with the sole purpose of achieving this for
her. This was only possible because she became clear
on where she wanted to be personally, professionally
and financially.

It did not take long for Janice's drawings to rocket and
her working hours to decrease as she shifted all the

businesses to the agreed end goal: prices went up, staff were recruited, difficult conversations held to unwind partnerships, underperforming assets sold and some of the entities shut down. A few months later, she moved to Australia and trained to get a real estate licence so she could realise her lifelong dream of selling properties in the sun. She now has a team in the UK, a budding business in Australia, all the money she needs and, most importantly, time with her family.

Establishing your finish line

When answering the question, *'Where are you going?'* it is always best to consider the answer from a personal perspective first and simply see your business as your chosen vehicle to get you there as quickly and effectively as possible. There are two main questions which we have alluded to previously that support this question:

1. How much do you want to draw from your business each month?

2. How many hours do you want to work to achieve this?

I encourage you to put the book down, get out your journal and work on both questions before you progress. Before you do, here are some guidelines to help you come up with high-value answers.

Guideline 1: Arbitrary targets mean arbitrary results

Most entrepreneurs set arbitrary targets and goals that mean nothing to them in practice. In the property industry, most new investors state they want to earn £10,000 a month, but when challenged, they need a lot less. When I first did this exercise, my number was £4,657 per month for my basic lifestyle and then £7,476 for my dream lifestyle. Even after becoming the sole provider and having kids, these figures have not changed much. Keep your figures meaningful. There should be no round numbers. Use real numbers that mean something to you.

You can find the template I use to calculate this here: www.ultimatefd.co.uk/small-business-big-profit/resources

Guideline 2: Remove limiting beliefs

When following the 'small business, big profit' methodology, it is possible to work as much or as little as you choose. My property business had ten team members, an office, a turnover over £500,000 per annum and I was sustaining this on 90 minutes a week. Rome was not built in a day and getting to this level may not happen in a year, but don't create a glass ceiling for yourself. You may be busy and not good at delegating, but put your target working hours down. Remember, nothing should ever be arbitrary. Make sure these hours mean something for you. Do they allow you to do the school run, go to the gym at lunchtime, or just generally get your evenings and weekends back?

Guideline 3: Design it so work can feel like play

Right now, your business may feel like a weight on your shoulders. It may be highly unprofitable and take a lot of personal sacrifices – I've been there and got a wardrobe of t-shirts to show for it. When you are in that position, your target working hours are normally close to zero, because you're burnt out, but the good news is that as your business turns and starts to pay you handsomely for the work you do, you will start to enjoy it again. Having worked with a lot of entrepreneurs and taken them on this journey, a sweet spot of between 20–30 hours per week seems to tick a lot of boxes.

Once you are clear on the income you want and how much time you want to invest, you can build a small business with high profits to achieve this. Clearly defining exactly what your business needs to look like is not as complicated as it may sound. In fact, keeping it simple is a key characteristic of a great business model. The output of the business model should be a business that kicks out surplus profit to allow you to achieve your desired level of drawings and have enough leverage in place to support your desired working hours.

6
Building Your Business Model For Success

The business model is the single difference between a business that is highly lucrative and one that barely breaks even. Every business needs a Bulletproof Business Model™ which consists of five simple rules that will govern the business. There may be a learning phase to begin with, particularly with brand new businesses where these are being amended and altered, but over time these rules will become embedded and, in most cases, will never change from the first £1 of revenue to the millionth! Here are the five simple rules you need to establish to form your model:

1. Profitable price: The price you will never drop below.

2. Profit per sale: A minimum profitability for each sale you make.

3. The profitability of your business: The minimum profit available for you to draw.

4. The sweet spot: A specific size that provides excellent service, minimal headaches and great profits.

5. Overhead budget: The maximum you can spend each month on running the business.

Once you have clearly defined these rules, they will act as guidelines that will allow you to know exactly what your business is going to look like once you follow them for a while. This is the end goal for the business, the answer to the question: *Where are you going*? To complete your Bulletproof Business Model while reading through this chapter, go to the link below to download the UFD Business Model template and input each of the five rules as you go: www.ultimatefd.co.uk/small-business-big-profit/resources

Principal rule: Don't break the rules

Above all the five rules is one overarching rule that you must never forget. *Don't break the rules!*

Recently, in a bid to get more sleep, my partner and I decided to sleep train our one-year-old. When she was a newborn she lost some weight, so we had to put her on a feeding plan and ensure she drank milk every three hours. This behaviour became habitual, and for the following eighteen months, she would wake up three to four times every night wanting milk. After reading up on the guidance and committing to a course, we learnt that one of the quickest ways to get more sleep was by taking away the night feeds, which seemed impossible at the time as there was no way she was going to sleep without milk.

To ease us in, they gave us a simple rule. No milk until 1am and then, if she is still asking for it, give her one bottle. Painful at first, but within around three days she was no longer interested in milk during the night. Two weeks later, she was sleeping from 7pm to 7am every day. Simple rule; a fundamental shift in results.

Your business has a set of nasty counterproductive habits created by you. Maybe you always discount to make a sale, you say yes whenever anyone asks for more money or a pay rise, you accept poor performance from team members because they have always been loyal or you put your savings in when the bank balance is low. These are all nasty habits, with nasty results.

Like the 1am rule, you need a set of similar rules to govern how you give your business the tough love it needs for the greater good. You do this by being explicitly clear as to how your business is going to work financially. Once you have a clear and defined set of financial rules, your business will naturally start to follow them and will be able to survive on you working fewer hours and not putting any money back in no matter how sparse the company account looks.

Rule 1: Profitable pricing

The first port of call is selecting a highly profitable price point for your services. Most entrepreneurs are pricing themselves broke and working far too hard to bring clients on board for low prices. Every sale feels like a win, but they are not charging enough to make those sales worthwhile, and in too many cases they would have been better off making no sales than making any at all.

The right price will result in some serious bottom-line profit for every sale and mean that you can keep your business small, achieving more profit than your counterpart who charges less, but must make double the amount of sales each month. Pricing is one of the most powerful tools in the entrepreneur's toolbox when it comes to big profits. Assuming that costs stay the same, increasing your price by as little as 10–15% has a dramatic impact on profit.

How do you select your pricing strategy? The Bullet Proof Business Model is answering the question: 'Where are you going?', so the price you input into the model will be an aspirational, yet realistic, minimum price point for you to work towards. Rather than trying to pick a number, you need to be aware of the three pricing strategies that are available to you and, based on the competitiveness in your industry, determine which one is realistic for you:

Strategy 1: Market-based pricing

This strategy involves simply pricing the same as everyone else does in your market. For example, we source property deals for £2,500 per deal, like everyone else. This is where most entrepreneurs start and too many stay. You can move away from this level by differentiating your service.

Strategy 2: Confidence-based pricing

When you have been in business long enough and you get to a stage where you have too many clients to service, you will naturally shift to confidence-based pricing. At this level, you charge above your competition because you know you do a better job. You may have an established brand, a better client process and a marketing budget to attract the right clients. All these elements allow you to charge a premium.

For example, my business not only sources the best deals, but we have sourced over a hundred deals in the last two years and currently have fifty-five-star Google reviews, so we can afford to be pricier than our competitors at £4,500 per deal.

This is a good level to be at; however, you are still exposed to the market and what your competitors are doing. Clients may be price sensitive and if your market-based competitors do drop their prices, you may need to do the same to maintain your sales. To move away from confidence, you must shift your focus from inwards to outwards and learn to productise.

Strategy 3: Problem-based pricing

At this level you do not sell services, you sell solutions. Your focus is to solve as many problems as you possibly can for your clients and be willing to get creative with as many different solutions as possible to do this for them. Your pricing should shift from how much time and resource is required to solve the problems for them to the value you create for them by uniquely solving their problems. The bigger the problem, the bigger the price.

For example, we renamed our generic deal sourcing service to the 'Hands-Free Deal Accelerator Programme' where we do everything for the client, including sourcing the deal, managing the buying process, completing a full refurbishment, setting up a lettings company, etc, all for just £12,000 per deal.

Problem-based pricing is set on the value you create, so the more value you create in monetary terms, the higher percentage of that value you can charge.

The further you can move along this spectrum away from market-based pricing and towards problem-based, the smaller your business can be with the highest level of profits. It can take time to develop a problem-based pricing model, so if you are currently at market, we would suggest inputting a confidence-based price into your model. Likewise, if you are confidence-based, think about how you could add more value to your clients and solve more problems.

SELLING SOLUTIONS

Perhaps the most impressive pricing journey I have witnessed is that of a good friend, Shiv Haria. Shiv started a property sourcing business in around 2016, charging market-based pricing of £2,500 per property sourced. In the first year they completed six deals in total. Shiv believed this was the maximum they could charge, as it was what everyone else was charging.

Over the years, confidence grew as they got more deals under their belt and had a lot of clients looking to work with them. They slowly increased prices to reduce the volume of clients that were approaching them as they could not cater for them all. Slowly and steadily the price crept to £3,500, then £4,500, then £5,995. Shiv could not quite believe that clients would be happy to pay this when their competitors were still selling similar deals at £2,500 per deal. As they made more money, Shiv started to improve the process and the team. He added additional features to their service, for example, a project management service to ensure the process was hands-free for the investors. They increased budgets for marketing materials, so everyone fully understood the sales journey while also developing their brand. Shiv started to shift his mindset to problem-solving and really understanding what the clients' problems were. At first, he thought the clients' problems were finding good returns, but over time, he realised this assumption was wrong and the main problem for these high net-worth individuals was a lack of time. He started to focus on making the service effortless, with minimal time input for the clients, thus maximising value for them.

Once again, they were getting too busy and coming close to having more clients than they could handle. Sales were easy and clients were paying in full in advance, so Shiv decided to do something bold: put his prices up a little every time he pitched to a client until someone said no. Over a few months, he kept pitching and everybody was still saying yes. It was not until his price reached £13,000 that prospective clients finally declined the price tag.

He was now doing sixty deals a year at £13,000 per deal, as opposed to six deals at £2,500, all because he had shifted his focus from market-based pricing to problem-based pricing.

 You can listen to Shiv's journey at: www.ultimatefd.co.uk/podcast-episodes/lucrative-leveraged-lifestyle-business[9]

---

9   J Keegan, 'Episode 68: Lucrative leveraged lifestyle business, with Shiv Haria', Ultimate FD podcast (4 June 2023), www.ultimatefd.co.uk/podcast-episodes/lucrative-leveraged-lifestyle-business, accessed 25 July 2023

Rule 2: Minimum profit per sale

As outlined previously, your gross margin is defined as the profitability of your product, unlike your net margin, which is the profitability of your business.

Gross margin is calculated by working out your price, less your cost of goods sold (which are the costs you incur to sell or deliver on a product or service). For example, if you own a bakery and sell cakes, the cost to make the cakes, including the raw ingredients (flour, eggs, butter, sugar) and the labour to make the cakes will be the cost of goods sold. If you sell the cake for £10 and the cost of ingredients was £5, then the difference between the two is your gross profit of £5.

You could make a rule that you always need to make £5 for every cake sold, but if you started selling wedding cakes for £500, then you would hope to make more than £5 for the expertise and skill required to deliver on this. Using a target percentage results in different levels of gross profit based on the price. For example, as a baker, you may target a 50% gross margin for every cake you make. This means that on your £10 cake you will make £5 gross profit and on your £500 wedding cake you will make £250 gross profit.

Maintaining a minimum gross margin is vital if you want to build a profitable business. It is influenced by two factors: the price charged and cost of goods sold. As an entrepreneur you are going to have to work hard on your business and having a minimum margin is the difference between working hard to get paid or working hard to go broke. There is a big difference between revenue and profitable revenue, and that difference is your gross margin.

You need to decide what your minimum gross margin is for every sale you make. Not only will this ensure that every sale you make is profitable, but it will also yield several additional benefits. Below are a few aspects to consider when setting your minimum gross margin.

Negotiations

The key to winning any negotiation is being clear on your minimum price point and being willing to walk away. When a prospective customer asks you to drop your price, one of the most powerful responses is: 'I'm sorry, but at that level, selling to you wouldn't make any financial sense to us. Of course, we would love to work with you, but the lowest we can go to is £...'

It puts a stake in the ground and your new client will likely respect the fact you have a minimum price point and know the value of your business, compared to a competitor who is willing to drive their price into the ground.

At an advanced level, I would advise you to create a discount table for new clients which outlines the discounts you can offer, but if you give anything extra in a negotiation, make sure you take something back. For example, 'The maximum discount we can offer you is 10%, assuming you sign a three-year contract,' or, 'We can offer you 15% off our normal price, but you will need to commit to giving us a Google review,' or, 'Yes, we can reduce the price by £1,000, assuming we get first refusal for your future projects,' etc. Work to your minimum margin when you need to win a strategically important client, but get rewarded for dropping your price.

Leverage

Having a minimum margin not only saves you time in negotiating, but also means you can empower your team to negotiate on your behalf. Provide a discount table and ensure they understand the lowest margin that they can drop to. They will then be able to negotiate independently, allowing you to take a step back from dealing with new clients.

Focus

You may have multiple product streams in the business: knowing your gross margin for each is crucial. Generally, focusing on the products or services with the higher margin will ensure you make more money than focusing on the ones that don't. It will also help you make decisions on what your business should and shouldn't do. If your current portfolio of services results in a minimum gross margin of 30%, it would not be wise to add a bolt-on service that would only generate a 10% gross margin as this would reduce the overall profitability of the business with the additional workload.

Working out the minimum gross margin per income stream you have and focusing on the higher ones is a sure-fire way to increase the profitability of your business.

Determining your gross margin

To determine your gross margin, simply input your existing cost of goods sold into your Bulletproof Business Model. Remember, these are the costs that are incurred because of an additional sale made. To go back to the baker's example, this would be the cost of ingredients for a cake.

You should now have a price, and a total cost to produce at that price, giving you a percentage margin. Your gross margin should be high. For service-based businesses, you would expect this to be at 60%+ and for product-based businesses at least 40%.

Rule 3: Profitability of the business

Understanding the difference between gross and net margin is essential for entrepreneurs and their future decision-making. Gross margin is the profitability of your product. Net margin is the profitability of your business. Two companies could be charging the same price and incur the same costs for each unit sold, meaning their gross margin is the same. This means that both sell equally profitable products, but few entrepreneurs run their businesses the same way, meaning the amount of money they may take home every month could be wildly different.

For example, Ultimate FD has two clients who are entrepreneurs that run letting agencies. They both charge a property management fee of 10% and have a rent roll of £200,000 per month, meaning their sales are £20,000 per month. The direct costs to manage the properties are small, but they have a few bits of software that charge on a per unit basis, plus marketing for each room, meaning they both have a gross margin of 75% and they both achieve a gross profit of £15,000.

However, while both agencies are run efficiently with a team of people, the key difference is that agency A has a physical office and a UK-based team costing £10,000 per month in total, whereas agency B allows all team members to work from home and has a team based in the Philippines costing £6,000 per month. Although both agencies have the same gross profit, their net profits are very different once the costs associated with running the business are factored in.

	A	B
Sales	20,000	20,000
Cost of Goods Sold	(5,000)	(5,000)
Gross Profit	15,000	15,000
Gross Margin	75%	75%
Overheads (Business running costs)	(10,000)	(6,000)
Net Profit	5,000	9,000
Net Profit Margin	25%	45%

The higher net margin percentage indicates a more efficient business making more profit with fewer sales. A high net margin is a desirable and fundamental part of any small business with big profits.

However, surprisingly few entrepreneurs focus on margin. They instead have tunnel-vision on sales or profit when margin is actually the most important financial metric in any business. I do not start or consider scaling a business unless the margin I can expect to achieve is 40%+, meaning that for every £1 of top-line revenue, I will be left with 40p profit. That is what I define as a lucrative business. To put this in perspective, the average net margin in the UK is between 8–15%,[10] although it's worth noting that to determine

---

10   Office for National Statistics, 'Profitability of UK companies: July to September 2022' (17 February 2023), www.ons.gov. uk/economy/nationalaccounts/uksectoraccounts/bulletins/ profitabilityofukcompanies/julytoseptember2022, accessed 24 August 2023

your target margin you should consider the type of business you operate:

- **Asset-backed businesses:** If your business is to buy or lease assets and generate income, for example from a rental portfolio, your margins are likely to be more like 10%, but some of our clients are still able to hit 20–30% for these businesses.

- **Product-based businesses:** Some product-based businesses initially have lower margins as they do not have the economies of scale to gain access to cost efficiencies. Margins can grow with time but vary greatly between industries.

- **Large businesses:** As a rule of thumb, the larger your business gets, the smaller the margin will be. Of course, you are looking at a smaller margin of a much larger turnover, but generally larger businesses make less bottom-line profit for each £1 of revenue (hence the title of this book).

So where is your net margin at? Input your target net margin figure based on the factors discussed above into your model alongside the revenue you believe you can achieve to determine your net margin percentage. We will be refining the model and the numbers where everything is inputted, so for now, if you need to put your finger in the air and hazard a guess, go for it, but be conservative. Remember that profit is a choice. We are striving for a finance-driven business and whatever you input will happen if it is driven by logic.

Rule 4: The profitable sweet spot

Businesses become more complicated the bigger they get. Unfortunately, you cannot expect a highly profitable and high-performing business to work as effectively if you grow it by 20%. Cracks will start to show and the well-oiled machine may start to crumble. Bigger is not always better and more revenue does not necessarily mean more profit. Growth tends to be most entrepreneurs' answer to everything. If you are not making enough money, you believe you need to be bigger and need more clients. If you are running out of cash, you think you need more sales. If your team is not performing well, you aim to grow to pay for a better team. The reality is that growth tends to exacerbate and compound all these problems and make things worse.

The aim of the game is to get your business to a 'sweet spot' as quickly as possible. A sweet spot is where three big factors come into perfect harmony: Client Service, Owner Leverage and Business Profitability. The diagram below illustrates how this all comes together.

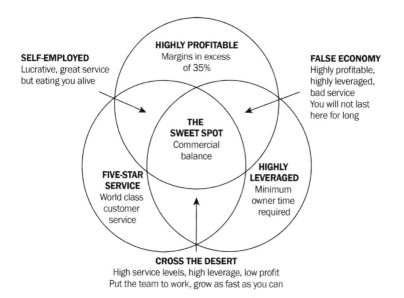

SELF-EMPLOYED
Lucrative, great service
but eating you alive

HIGHLY PROFITABLE
Margins in excess
of 35%

FALSE ECONOMY
Highly profitable,
highly leveraged,
bad service
You will not last
here for long

**THE
SWEET SPOT**
Commercial
balance

**FIVE-STAR
SERVICE**
World class
customer
service

**HIGHLY
LEVERAGED**
Minimum
owner time
required

CROSS THE DESERT
High service levels, high leverage, low profit
Put the team to work, grow as fast as you can

The challenges of not being in a sweet spot

When you're not in a sweet spot, you're in a danger
zone and will normally be experiencing some sort of
pain/stress according to that zone. Below I've outlined the zones you might find yourself in and what
you need to tackle before hitting the sweet spot:

- **False economy:** If you have a 'highly profitable'
  business with high leverage, you may be making
  a lot of money with your team doing most of the
  work for you. In a sense, you have made it as an
  entrepreneur. However, if you neglect service
  levels and these slip, then before you know it
  profits can start to dip and you get pulled back

into the day-to-day workings of the business.
If you are enjoying a 'false economy' right now,
I would suggest jumping back in and getting
your hands dirty to sort your service before you
are forced to.

- **Self-employed:** Entrepreneurs who experience
  high profits and deliver great service with
  minimal leverage generally do the work
  themselves. This is more a job than a business,
  in that your income stops if you stop doing the
  work. A lot of us start here, but it is a dangerous
  place to be as you risk both burnout and an
  income ceiling (the only way to earn more is for
  you to work more and your time is finite). You
  can move away from being self-employed to
  owning a business by getting a team in place.

- **Cross the desert:** If your service is great meaning
  you have lots of leverage in your team but no profit
  as you are paying for that team, then you need to
  'cross the desert'. Grow quickly but keep the same
  level of capacity. We call this 'crossing the desert'
  because the zone you are currently in is highly
  risky, so you want to do this as quickly as you can.
  All it takes is for you to lose a client or have a dip
  in sales and you go from a small profit to a loss.
  Considered growth is required to get you to the
  sweet spot and add more profit to the business.

- **Making trade-offs:** There will always be trade-
  offs to get to the sweet spot. Service may never be
  as good as when you were doing it yourself and

responding to every customer email that comes in at 11pm. Your leverage may not be quite as high when you cross the desert and add more clients or sales to your existing team. Profits may go down in the short term when you start to invest in service. The first port of call is to accept these trade-offs and get to the sweet spot, then once you are there you can work on every part to improve it and over time trade-offs will be minimal.

What to consider when you grow

Profitable businesses do not grow linearly. They step change, and at certain sweet spots they are profitable. There are two considerations to bear in mind when you decide to grow:

1. Is the next sweet spot worth it? If you are currently making £6,000 per month in your business and you only need £5,000, do you want to risk it all to get to the next sweet spot, which may be £15,000 per month profit? Maybe you do, but there are often much easier ways to earn similar money than to grow, for example, introducing additional revenue streams which keep the business the same size but exponentially increase profitability.

2. Are you confident that the next sweet spot will be all it is cracked up to be? You need to be sure that the mechanics will work at the next sweet spot before you grow, otherwise, you may have

to experience one to three years of painful growth with a less profitable business to show for it.

So many good businesses are destroyed by ill-considered growth. Here's a simple example to demonstrate.

THE TALE OF THE BARBER[11]

A young man moves to a village and realises he must travel miles to get a decent haircut, so he decides to set up a barbershop. He can manage two hundred haircuts a week if he works long hours. He is not aware of the external need, but the demand in the market is five hundred cuts per week.

He opens the shop and gets off to a slow start, but soon he has people queuing out of the door to get their haircuts. The phone is constantly ringing and he cannot keep up with the high demand in the marketplace. He decides to bring on another barber to add capacity to the shop and service more clients. They can now service four hundred haircuts a week, but the market demand is still five hundred.

The phone is still ringing and people are still queuing out the door and even leaving because they do not want to wait that long, so the young man takes the logical next step. He brings in a third barber so they can now service six hundred haircuts a week.

---

11   This analogy is from Property Entrepreneur, Daniel Hill, www. property-entrepreneur.co.uk

For the first few weeks they are all swamped and working overtime, evenings and weekends to service the pent-up demand, but then suddenly, something happens. There is no more queue at the door. The phone stops ringing and the three barbers go from cutting hair all day to having extended lunch breaks, finishing early on a Friday and getting their evenings and weekends back. The employees are chuffed, but the owner isn't. He's now paying for two additional barbers to sit around for half of the day. He sees his profits drop and, although his revenue has never been higher, he is now making significantly less money. Not sure why this has happened, he starts investing in some expensive marketing: social media ads, flyers, etc, and reducing prices in a bid to get busy again, thus reducing profits further.

If the young man had done his research, he would have known that what happened was that they created too much capacity for the market. The market demand was five hundred haircuts a week, and they had created a surplus capacity of six hundred. They went from being oversubscribed with a queue of clients at the door to being underworked and spending additional money on marketing to solve the problem.

This example may seem simplistic, but most entrepreneurs are constantly behaving like the barbershop. When the business is working well, they assume that if they increase capacity by a third, then profits will increase by the same. Unfortunately, this is rarely the case.

The sweet spot for the barber would have been to keep capacity for four hundred haircuts, put prices up and never have to worry about spending any money on marketing. This is where the business would have been highly profitable. Once prices were higher, the barber may also have been able to recruit someone to replace himself to achieve more leverage.

Find a sweet spot where demand is in surplus, push up your prices and save your marketing budget. Remember: small business = big profits.

Now input your sweet spot size into your Bulletproof Business Model. How big can you get to be profitable, offer five-star service and achieve leverage?

Rule 5: The overhead budget

The final piece of the puzzle is your overhead budget. Fortunately, there is not too much work for you to do here if you have followed the previous four rules.

First off, you need to be clear on what you must spend each month to run the business. These are fixed costs which do not deviate with sales. For example, office costs, salaries, monthly contractor invoices, accounting costs, tax accountants, software subscriptions, insurance, etc.

I've explained the difference between gross margin and net margin (gross being the profitability of your product and net being the profitability of your business). This means that two businesses can have the same gross margin, but very different net margins, and the difference is the cost of the monthly over-heads used to run the business. The good news is that managing overheads is simple. Set a budget and stick to it. As your business gets bigger you may find you need to increase that budget, which is fine, but be sure to review it at least annually and make changes in line with where you are at.

In a finance-driven business, you decide everything else first, such as what price you are going to charge and how much money you are going to make, and once that is done you will be left with an overhead budget that you just have to make work. The more scarce the budget, the more efficient the business needs to be. I have seen entrepreneurs build incred-ible businesses with minimal overheads by investing in systems and utilising the arbitrage of cheaper inter-national labour markets.

If you are inputting your business into the Bulletproof Business Model template,[12] you will see the model has now calculated overheads for you. Here is the logic around the calculation:

Revenue [price × sweet spot] (Rules 1 and 4)

Minus: Cost of sales (Rule 2) = gross profit

Minus: Overheads = net profit (Rule 3)

---

12   You can find a copy of this template here: www.ultimatefd.co.uk/ small-business-big-profit/resources

Since we have all the parts of the equation (apart from overheads, if you do net profit − gross profit), you now have your budget. For example:

Rule 1 (price per sale): £1,000

Rule 2 (cost of goods sold): £400

Rule 3 (target net margin): 35%

Rule 4 (sweet spot): 10 sales a month

Revenue (monthly): £10,000 (£1,000 × 10)

Cost of goods sold: £4,000 (£400 × 10)

Gross profit: £6,000 (£10,000 − £4,000)

Overheads: TBC

Net profit: £3,500 (£10,000 × 35%)

Based on the above example, with gross profit being £6,000 and net profit being £3,500, our overhead budget of £2,500 per month is the difference.

Right now, you just need to know what your overhead budget is. We will talk through how you allocate this later in the book, particularly as you may not be at your business sweet spot yet, so you may not have the full budget to spend. I would encourage you to now sense check and 'play' with the Bulletproof Business Model. If, for example, that overhead budget looks far too low, can you increase your pricing? Can you make more sales every month? Can you reduce your minimum net profit? Although we want the sweet spot to be lucrative, it is incredibly important that it is realistic, so 'play' with each of the input variables until you get to a point where the business is ticking all the boxes.

Part Two: Summary

Now, maybe for the first time, you have crystal-clear clarity on where your business is heading and where it will work well as a business and as an owner. You have five rules and if you stick to them your finances will almost take care of themselves.

This is a huge milestone, and it is rare that entrepreneurs ever get away from arbitrary growth targets and scaling unprofitable businesses, so congratulations! You now know where you are and where you are going, but there is a missing link: How do you get there? I wish we could just click our fingers and have a perfect business overnight but it can take anywhere from six months to two years to build a Bulletproof Business.

This is where you need to get strategic and take it to another level. Part Three is your insurance policy and the difference between coming up with a plan and achieving it. Let's dive in and answer the question: How do you get there?

PART THREE
HOW DO YOU GET THERE?

7
Meet Your Future Forecast™

For the final section, I'd like to tell you about serial property entrepreneurs Mo Haykir and James Yorke.

MOORVIEW LETS

Mo and James have multiple property businesses, including a letting agency, several property holding companies and a multi-million-pound development company. Their businesses and portfolios were achieving seven-figure revenues across the group. However, although the companies and businesses were growing, their personal incomes weren't. In fact, often they were required to reinvest any hard-earned cash back into the business.

They had already cracked the first two questions with a finance team in place to provide monthly management accounts answering, *Where are we now?* And, in theory, they knew where they were going for each entity, confidently sharing growth targets and minimum margins, thus answering the question: *Where are you going?* However, year after year they just could not seem to reach the sweet spot they were striving for. Instead, they were dealing with daily emergencies, recruiting team members whenever the other team members said they were too busy, growing as much as they could and spending unlimited amounts to reach their targets. Every year they decided that this would be the year it finally worked and be able to justify why, and then the same again: some progress, but generally costs increasing more than revenue.

They knew what the end goal was, but they hadn't broken that goal down into a comprehensive, realistic, step-by-step financial plan. Like most entrepreneurs, they felt overwhelmed by the concept of pulling this plan together, so wrote a few bits down but glossed over a lot of the details and decided that they would work it out as they went.

They worked with Ultimate FD to get their first twelve-month forecast, called a Future Forecast, in place for each of their businesses. For the first time, not only did they have their end goal, but they had a highly realistic step-by-step, monthly financial plan to get them from where they were to where they wanted to get to.

Like most entrepreneurs, they have never had an issue with executing, they just needed the right plan to follow. They recruited team members as planned. When their existing teams asked for pay rises, they said, 'No, that's not in the budget, but we can discuss it next year.' They relentlessly executed to hit their monthly sales target. Every single one of their team members knew exactly what was expected of them each month. They introduced new revenue streams in line with the forecast. They cut the costs in the timeframes they promised they would. They took money from the companies as they planned, bringing more stability to their personal finances.

As if by magic, in their first year they had their most profitable year on record. The profit they made across the group was within £150 of what they had forecast. Three years on, and after producing a Future Forecast each year, they now have one of the most profitable letting agencies I have ever seen and each of their other businesses now kicks out healthy drawings for them every month. What's more, they now work a fraction of the time to maintain over ten times their previous drawings.

Your best financial year on record is born from your best financial plan on record. Mo and James would now never start a financial year without a comprehensive Future Forecast with every stone unturned for every entity, and neither should you!

 You can listen to Mo and James' story here: www. ultimatefd.co.uk/podcast-episodes/zero-to-hero[13]

---

13   J Keegan, 'Episode 38: Zero to hero, with Mo Haykir', Ultimate FD podcast (23 October 2022), www.ultimatefd.co.uk/podcast-episodes/zero-to-hero, accessed 25 July 2023

It's time to plan your journey

You know where you are, you are clear on where you are going, and now it is time to work out how you get there. Very few entrepreneurs ever create a comprehensive financial plan, and so they rarely achieve any long-term financial success. They may have a good month, or a good quarter, but then six months of financial difficulties. To build a business with big profits, you need to have a big profit plan. Profit is highly predictable, but never easy.

You need to know what you need to do by when. How many sales do you need to get next month? What does your minimum gross margin need to be? When do you recruit that virtual assistant? When are you implementing that new system? This is the road-map for taking you from where you are to where you want to be.

The best practice is to make all these decisions upfront and then to check in with the forecast monthly to hold yourself accountable. I appreciate it can be difficult for some business owners to think more than twelve hours ahead, let alone twelve months, but the ability to plan and be proactive is one of the single most powerful tools in your entrepreneurial toolbox. The alternative is to show up every day and just make the decisions that feel right at the time. Are you going to be able to say no to a team member's pay rise request when the idea of them leaving keeps you up at night? Are you going to implement a system which you know will save you time when you are already so busy? Are you going to cut the costs you said you would when it is easier not to? Are you going to do what you know is right when there is a much easier, less resistant path on the table in the heat of the moment?

In a finance-driven business, all the financial decisions are decided in advance and the business must dance to your tune, not the other way around. This is how you achieve a level of calm, clarity and confidence as an entrepreneur and stay on track when everything around you is crumbling. This is how you have your best financial year on record, every year!

I'm excited to introduce you to the tool you need to answer the question: *How do you get there?* Meet the Future Forecast.

Every entrepreneur needs a very simple, yet comprehensive working model of their business which allows them to create a plan for at least the following twelve months and allows them to 'play' with all the different scenarios they are considering, including new lines of business or growth targets. Previously, we talked about the business model and the rules you are going to follow. The Future Forecast breaks this journey down to get that model into a month-by-month plan.

Key benefits to having a Future Forecast

The benefits you will experience as an entrepreneur when you have this in place are endless. Getting the Future Forecast right puts the power back into the hands of the business owner and allows more confidence to make the right changes. Let's take a look at the three key benefits to having a Future Forecast in place:

Benefit 1: One bite at a time

The saying goes, 'How do you eat an elephant? One bite at a time.' Your plans over the next twelve months will probably feel massive to you. As is often the case, motivation can be high at the start, but as the challenges start to set in this can drop and discipline is needed to keep going. There is always a risk of experiencing overwhelm, which can be crippling for progress. There are also always good and bad months. The key is to break it all down into manageable monthly actions – small chunks that you can do and feel proud of, and which, added together, build towards your final, bigger goal.

Benefit 2: No stone unturned

By committing to make a robust twelve-month Future Forecast, you will inherently leave fewer stones unturned than you ever have before. It will encourage you to answer questions about the 'how' that you might usually put off and you could find that it's these unturned stones that cause the stress and risks to your plan and financial success. There may always be parts of the year that you don't know until you get there, or surprises that crop up, but by aiming for an 80:20 approach (with 80% being planned and 20% being unknown), you are 80% more likely to have your best year on record.

Benefit 3: Massive accountability

If I was granted one wish, I believe the most dramatic self-improvement wish would be: I wish that whenever I say I am going to do anything I always do it, no matter what. Think about the power that would have. No missed gym sessions. Always hitting 10k steps a day. Only eating healthy food. Stopping at one alcoholic drink. Getting up at 5am. Reading a book a week. Never using your phone in front of your kids. Always being on time. Hitting any goal you set for yourself. The reality is that we are our own worst enemy and every year I work with hundreds of entrepreneurs that all know the battle is won if they just do what they say they are going to do. After genies and spells, the second-best tool for making things happen is black-and-white accountability.

Your Future Forecast will become embedded into your business and is the ultimate accountability tool keeping you in check. Have you done what you said you were going to do? If you are now behind on sales and haven't made the recruits you said you would, what are you going to do now to bring in the plan? The Future Forecast keeps you in check. It is the difference between going to the gym by yourself, or with a personal trainer encouraging you and counting every rep. Which method do you think gets better results?

8
Clients, Capacity and Cash

There are three key elements to building out your Future Forecast and giving you the roadmap you need to build your dream business: Clients, Capacity and Cash. We will go through each part so you can build out the Future Forecast. You may not have all the answers now, but build it and then schedule some time to play with it until you get to where you need to be.

Clients

In an ideal world, growth would be linear and predictable, but in the real world, growth takes time and tends to be more of a J-curve, particularly for a business that is new to the market. This causes issues from a financial perspective as there may be increased costs initially, with revenue coming in later, meaning a lagging impact on profit. None of this is a problem if you know what it will look like and have a well-considered sales forecast broken down into quarters. Sales result in money coming into the business, thus allowing everything else to keep functioning, so the key when forecasting new sales is to be prudent, realistic and aware of seasonality.

In your Future Forecast there are two types of sales to consider: existing business and new business. You likely already have clients that you are working with which will need to be forecasted into the model. You might create a line for each client and detail income expected for them, or if they are all roughly the same, you could create a line specifically for all existing clients. Assuming you have your WCFF set up, getting this information should be easy and it will help you make assumptions about new clients based on the ones you are already working with.

Existing business is already committed to working with you, but remember that unless a contract has been signed, or at least a deposit paid, you do not want to add these to your forecast. A sales forecast should always be prudent, so only include sales that you know are 100% committed. If the only commitment you have is the spoken word or a handshake, then leave them out of the existing business forecast for now.

The next type to consider is your new business. These are clients that are planning to work with you or potential new business that you are going to bring on. You might not know yet who the clients are, or what the business deal will look like, so you need to create a forecast based on how many of these new clients have a high probability of paying you over the next twelve months. You should already know the quantity of new clients you need after completing your Bulletproof Business Model, so now it is a case of planning the growth. For instance, if on average for every ten leads you receive you secure one new client, then you can figure out how many sales calls/leads need to be generated to hit those targets. Of course, the quicker you can get these clients on board the better, but sales can be more of a J-curve and your year may be backloaded.

There are a couple of considerations for forecasting new business that are worth taking into account:

1. **Under-promise, overdeliver:** A great sales forecast is a prudent one. Keep the numbers smaller than what you would want. Grow slower than you would like and aim to overdeliver on your targets. By doing this, you are naturally adding two important elements into your forecast that will dramatically increase its value. First, realism. Sales are always more difficult than we think they are going to be. How many entrepreneurs do you know that hit

their growth targets for the year, every year? Likely very few. Second, motivation. By creating a sales forecast you can beat, you keep up motivation throughout the year rather than sinking under the pressure of being so far behind enormous targets.

Under-promising, overdelivering is key with any goal setting and has a monumental impact on motivation. Business is all a game, and it is much more enjoyable to be winning than losing. Next to my desk, there is a whiteboard that currently has 'Overachieved £14,223' written on it. This motivates me as each day when I sit down at my desk I am reminded of the wins of the business. My target could have been £20,000 higher, but instead of feeling like a success, the mindset would feel very different. Same financial result, but very different motivation levels.

2. **Seasonal sales:** Many businesses have a seasonal period where sales are high, and a down period where sales are low. In a lot of industries, these align with the actual seasons (retail and Christmas aside, of course). For instance, in property, people tend to buy more houses, sell more houses and look to move in the summer, so if you are an estate agent or construction firm this will likely be your busiest season for sales.

Identify when your high sales season is and forecast more in this period than the others. Once you have that in place you can focus your marketing campaigns on the time when the potential for new revenue is at a peak. Be realistic about quiet seasons. Setting high ambitions during your down period is likely just setting yourself up to fail.

Once you have a forecast for your client growth you must now execute relentlessly and make it happen. No more just focusing on sales when you have the time or feel like it or selling all the time. Get strategic with client acquisition and growth. Clients mean revenue, which is the top of the funnel that feeds the entire machine. You cannot afford to get behind on sales, so every single month and quarter work out exactly how you are going to hit your growth targets and make it happen.

Too many entrepreneurs have clear sales targets for the year, but forget a key detail which is vital for delivering on them: capacity. It is important to get the balance between growth and capacity right, otherwise you risk growing yourselves broke or increasing the cost base at a level that outpaces the sales.

Capacity

Let's talk about overhead budgets. Your end goal might be to have a generous overhead budget that allows for a trendy office space and the latest computers, but this is for once you've gotten to the financial place you aimed for. On the way to this, you are going to have to work with what you have available.

If you spend more than you have, then you may get yourself into significant financial difficulty. You need to get strategic with capacity and, more importantly, when you decide to leverage elements of the business as you grow. By inputting your sales forecast into the model, you will now have a monthly overhead budget to allocate to each month over the full year. This budget might even be given the freedom to expand as the business grows. But for now, we have two questions: What are we going to spend the budget on? When are we going to make spending changes?

Before we dive in, when we talk about overheads, these are costs that are fixed and essential to run the business, for example, an office lease or a salary. Of course, these costs can change and are not fixed forever, but they do not vary with sales (ie, they are not related to the cost of acquisition). The aim is to keep the overhead budget as low as possible while keeping the business running efficiently and reducing the time required from you as the entrepreneur.

Five overhead categories

There are five overhead categories that must be considered and forecasted:

1. **Salaries:** Salaries often make up a large part of the overhead budget, even with a small team running the business. You need to decide which recruits are essential and when they will be needed to manage the client forecast you have created. In the early days, you may opt for virtual assistants, then evolve to full-time employees when ready.

2. **Rent and office costs:** Increasingly fewer businesses must forecast rent and office costs as working styles have evolved to become more remote. Of course, you may still have an office depending on your business type, and this needs to be forecasted alongside any office equipment such as printers.

3. **Marketing and sales:** Every business needs a marketing and sales budget. Your marketing budget could be flexible and based on performance or a monthly set amount, such as in the case of paying an agency retainer. However, sales costs can be less consistent and you should use your sales forecast to work backwards to what you want to be spending each month on sales campaigns.

4. **Accounting and finance:** Generally business owners can expect to spend 1–3% of revenue on this area. Of course, if you have not already set up your WCFF from Part One of this book, be sure to add in the forecasted costs of

doing this. However, don't forget to add your tax accountant's retainer.

5. **Systems and software:** A great business is run on great systems and software. Work out all the systems you will need and add them all into this line. Be generous here – great systems can dramatically reduce your salaries budget.

Spending options

You are hopefully now getting the gist that it is not enough to just decide what you are going to spend, but you also need to decide the 'when'. There are three options for this:

1. **Emergency spend capacity:** Most entrepreneurs take this route: only increasing overheads from a position of pain. When everything is breaking around them, they finally bite the bullet and make a recruit or implement a new system. This is a highly reactive approach and never allows you to get back into the driver's seat as you're always firefighting.

2. **Real-time spend capacity:** Rather than letting things break or go too far wrong, this option recruits based on capacity requirements at the time. For instance, you are aware that next month you will be taking on an extra fifteen clients, so you have started the process now to bring on a new system or a team member to cover this

increased need. This is a much better approach than the emergency capacity style, but will still create a high-stress environment as lining up capacity with sales will be a continuous challenge which will never be quite right. However, if you are on a tight financial shoestring, this can be necessary as the cash reserves needed to recruit or bring on overheads earlier than you need to are not available.

3. **Forward funding:** This approach is advanced and is about taking on excess capacity ahead of time, getting it all primed and then explosively growing to utilise it. This is the ultimate method used by advanced entrepreneurs and allows the fullest level of leverage. You bring on the team, the systems and all the costs you will need before you need them, and then you grow into this capacity. There are, of course, risks around having overheads before sales from a financial perspective, but if you are confident and strategic then those risks are insignificant to the benefits of accelerated growth when not being limited by capacity.

Now it is time to allocate your overheads throughout the year and address your strategic issues around capacity. Make sure that when you allocate capacity, it is in line with your peaks of sales activity so you can be successful in delivering on that growth. Similar to the philosophy about forecasting your sales, I would recommend allocating all your available overhead budget, even if you do not think you will need it. Remember, the aim is to be prudent and set yourself up with a forecast you can beat!

In summary, you should now have a month-by-month growth plan and know what you are going to spend, and by when, to deliver on that growth. You should also have a fully mapped out P&L, and an idea of exactly how much money you will make over the next twelve months (more specifically, what you can expect to make in each individual month ongoing). You may want to allocate time to 'play' with the numbers to rework it to a level that suits your ambitions for the year ahead, for example, bringing some sales forwards so you can make some recruits earlier.

There is now only one piece of the puzzle missing, and it's a big piece. Cash. Earlier in the book I emphasised the importance of cash. By completing the Future Forecast for profit, you have an incredible starting point and more clarity than most entrepreneurs ever get. However, you now need to take this to the next level and forecast cash over the next twelve months.

Cash

It was not until I ran out of cash that I understood why seasoned entrepreneurs say that 'Cash is king'. You can have a highly profitable business, but still have major cash issues. Cash is holistic and covers everything that the P&L does not. For example, your Future Forecast may not consider your dividend drawings as these are a cash item. If you are set to make £120,000 per year as profit, but are aiming to draw £140,000 as dividends, you are going to have cash issues. Corporation tax is a cash item, normally paid around nine months after the current year to HMRC, so you may have a large chunk of money going out that would not appear in your P&L. If you decide to forward-fund your business, you will need more cash than you have profit to get started. If your business is an asset-based business like a property portfolio, then for every bit of growth there may be a large capital expenditure that you need to factor in.

As long as you have a Bulletproof Business Model and do not overdraw/spend money owed to HMRC, then cash issues can often be solved by managing the timings of inflows and outflows. This is why the cash element of the Future Forecast is vital. It is this that will allow you to spot problems before they become emergencies and alter plans to ensure you stay in the black.

Once you have put in the groundwork shared in this book, forecasting cash flow becomes a far more simplistic exercise. Your WCFF gives you insight into previous cash trends and allows you to verify expected future trends. The Bulletproof Business Model gives you an endpoint and position to aim for. The bottom-line net profit figure on the completed

Future Forecast gives you the top line in the cash flow forecast called 'net cash from operations', which is the amount of cash you can expect to have left over at the end of each month.

Additional cash items

Next, it's time to add additional cash items based on what you already know about. The problem most entrepreneurs face is this is in their heads, so the first job is to get it all out onto the record. Below are some major cash items to factor in:

1. **Drawings:** How much are you going to take from the business each month? Note that the mechanism for taking drawings is not important at this stage and your tax accountant can advise on the most tax-efficient way for you to draw what you want. For now, enter how much you would like to draw month by month. If you are not sure, I would always recommend not setting these too high; while it can be tempting to consistently take out as much as you can every month, you never want to be in a position where you must put back in. Set a lower drawing target that can always be achieved, for example, 50% of net profit, then pay yourself a quarterly bonus based on what you have achieved if you want extra. You may also want to include any savings and investment schemes here, for example, paying into ISAs or pensions.

2. **Debt:** Forecast any money you may need to take in the form of debt or any money you intend to pay back. Make sure you include interest if this is rolled up to the final repayment. Include credit cards and any consumer debt here too, particularly if you already have it in place.

3. **Investments:** Include any investments outside the realms of your normal P&L. For example, you may decide to buy an office, investment property or Bitcoin. Whatever it is, put it in here.

4. **Tax:** Corporation tax and VAT are the most important lines here. Of course, if you are not VAT registered you do not need to forecast VAT, but there is nothing worse than an unexpected figure on your corporation tax bill. Keep it simple and calculate this by multiplying your expected profit by the corporation tax rate and enter when you can expect it to be paid.

5. **Additional (one-offs):** Finally, a section for any larger, one-off items for any cash flows that are outside of normal business.

Once you have added all the above to your cash flow forecast, you should now be getting a very clear picture of what the next year will look like for you from a cash perspective. Remember, knowing you are going to need more cash in a few months is not stressful, but not knowing and finding out that you need it tomorrow is highly stressful!

Achieving cash positive

Your Future Forecast should have greens or reds based on cash positive or cash negative (respectively). You now need to plug the gap so it all becomes green. There are three ways you can do this:

1. **Change the timing:** The first port of call is to alter cash timing. Can you bring the cash in faster and push the cash spending dates out further? Will a lender accept being paid back three months later? Will a big client pay for a year's worth of work upfront for a small discount? Can you balance transfer your credit card and get 0% interest to pay it back nine months later? What can you move around to balance the books and get more greens than reds?

2. **Tweak and tinker:** Probably one of the most enjoyable parts of having a Future Forecast is the ability to play around with the inputs and answer the 'what-ifs?' If the output is not what you want it to be, why don't you see what happens if you make some more sales this year, increase your prices and take slightly less out in the form of drawings? What happens if you commit to one new recruit instead of two? What happens if you move out of the office and invest in a system for people to work from home? Play around with the inputs and see if you can keep the bank balance above zero.

3. **Raise the money:** In some cases, there may be holes that cannot be filled without external finance, so the third option is to decide when you are going to raise the money and at what level. Raising money to grow your business should not be considered a bad thing, just ensure that the interest is plugged into your cash flow forecast as well as planning ahead for getting the finance paid back.

Cash is often the missing piece of the puzzle and a highly important one. As your business starts to perform well, cash flow should be where your primary focus is. Throughout the Future Forecast, every element you change will kick in changes further down the model. Add one more sale in and watch your cogs increase, gross profit go up, as well as your net profit and your cash position. An increase in overheads will trigger a decline in both net profit as well as your net cash. As you start to realise the impact one has on another, you can understand the system more fully. Once you understand the system, you can then master the game!

9
What Now?

You have clarity, a goal and know how to get there, so what now? We have all had that diet plan we never followed, that business plan we never read, or that brilliant idea we never did anything about. There's always a risk in business that your hard work does not pay off or that you stray so far from what you set out to do that it's a struggle to get back.

A close friend and highly accomplished entrepreneur shared with me that he once spent £10,000 on a business forecast that he never used. This book aims to not only stress how important it is for you to understand exactly how to make your finance function and forecasts work, but also how to extract the most value from them so they become a game-changer for your business.

The Future Forecast should hold you entirely accountable for your actions and keep you on track when you are veering off. It needs to be the ultimate accountability tool that is constantly pushing you to do uncomfortable, high-effort activities that ensure you achieve what you want to achieve. There are four cornerstones you now need to set up to make this happen.

Cornerstone 1: Greens and reds

The first cornerstone is your 'greens and reds'. When you now review your Three Pillars with your team of four professionals at your monthly milestone, greens and reds will level up the way your finances are run and the quality of conversations you have. Green indicates a line is ahead of budget, meaning you are making more sales than forecast or your costs are less than expected. Red indicates the opposite. Understand the greens and what got them there and seek to take action to change the reds to greens. The easiest way to do this is to revisit your forecast and check whether you are doing what you said you should be.

Over time, as your finance manager starts to learn your business, they should be able to add commentary for any variances over 5%, making the review process even better. Don't underestimate the value of understanding the reds and seeking to change them. I appreciate that new deals and clients are a lot more fun to dwell on, but most of your profit will be unlocked by keeping your reports overwhelmingly green.

Cornerstone 2: Quarterly goals

The next cornerstone is summarised brilliantly in the book *The 12 Week Year: Get More Done in 12 Weeks than Others Do in 12 Months*[14] by Brian P Moran. The concept is simple. Breaking a big annual goal into smaller quarterly goals is much more motivating, because the time horizon is far shorter. It is also easier to quantify what can be achieved and what needs to be done in a shorter timeframe than planning for an entire year.

You now have a new way of goal setting, and that is setting goals based on the forecast. For example, I tend to set a 'Quarterly Top Three', which are high-value business goals that must be achieved above all else. For a long time, these came from my head and what I felt was right at the time, but now they come from the Future Forecast. In Q2, if you are due to recruit a sales progressor, then make that a goal. If you need to do a big sales campaign in Q3, make that your goal. If you are due to launch a new product or line of business in Q4, make that one of your top three. In a finance-driven business, the forecast tells you what to do and then the numbers follow. Don't just set goals

---

14 BP Moran, *The 12 Week Year: Get More Done in 12 Weeks than Others Do in 12 Months* (Wiley, 2013)

based on how you are feeling at the time; check into your forecast whenever you are setting any goals, be that quarterly, monthly or even weekly.

Cornerstone 3: Tangible targets

The third cornerstone is one you will already be familiar with – tangible targets. For potentially the first time, you should now have a robust set of targets. You know what your sales target is for Q2. You know what your gross margin target is. Now it's time for action. The first step is to roll the targets out for the rest of the business to see. Then, for the areas you are responsible for, get yourself a whiteboard that you update weekly to hold yourself accountable. For other targets, communicate these clearly with the team member who will be responsible for them and create a scorecard they can update weekly to track progress.

Once you have a set of tangible targets that are communicated throughout your business, the weight of the sole responsibility for the business's performance will finally come off your shoulders and become a shared role.

Cornerstone 4: General meetings

And finally, the last cornerstone – general meetings. One of the most productive types of meeting you can have is a general meeting, often called a Quarterly General Meeting (QGM) or Annual General Meeting (AGM), depending on when it is held. I'd recommend not waiting to have one a year, but to hold one of these every three months to sign off the last quarter and kick off the new one. It is the perfect time to dive into and update the Future Forecast in line with any significant changes that have happened or any assumptions that may change the future.

In huge businesses, changing a forecast is challenging as this would require updating the expected company performance and communicating amends to shareholders. Fortunately, in smaller businesses, changing a forecast is not challenging and can be highly valuable. Remember, the Future Forecast answers the question: How do I get there? If you take a few wrong turns on your journey, you now need a new route to get to your planned destination. Changing this on a whim is not acceptable, but formally changing it quarterly with all relevant stakeholders is advised. Make reviewing and updating the Future Forecast a key part of your quarterly general meetings and part of your annual calendar.

Part Three: Summary

The third and final part of this book tackles the big question: How do you get there? With the financial clarity you've gained from parts one and two on where your business is now and where it is heading, you are now equipped with everything you need to map out your journey to achieve big profit.

In this section you have met the Future Forecast, the key to getting strategic and taking your business to another level. This section explores how to make financial decisions in advance, so your profit becomes highly predictable. As part of this, you have also met the three Cs: Clients, Capacity and Cash – the key elements to building your finance-driven business.

In the final chapter, What Now?, you discovered how you can bring it all together and put this newfound financial clarity and road map to work to maximise the value you get as well as your business' performance. Now it is time to draw the book to a conclusion.

10
Conclusion

Daring to be small will require a big mindset shift. Growing a business comes naturally to many entrepreneurs, but designing a highly lucrative small business which gives you all the income you need while matching your ideal lifestyle/working hours requires dedication to that end goal. Entrepreneurs who have finally seen the light and have switched to the 'small business, big profit' mindset are calm and collected and have time to enjoy the work they do as well as more profit to withdraw.

Being financially literate and diligent in every decision is non-optional for success in this approach. In this book, I have taken you through the three key questions you need to get to grips with to shift into a finance-driven business. The starting point was,

'Where are you now?' and you gained this clarity by implementing the World Class Finance Function. This means you should now know all the numbers crucial to your business and have a carefully selected finance team to manage these figures every month.

Next, you will have decided what 'good' looks like for you personally by answering the question, 'Where are you going?' Here, the Bulletproof Business Model steps in and helps create a set of simple rules that you can now live by; guides for your minimum prices and maximum overheads, with the most important rule being, 'Don't break the rules'.

Finally, the last step of the journey was answering the question, 'How do you get there?' You should now have a Future Forecast with targets outlining what you need to do by when and providing accountability that will force you to make these targets a reality.

Now all you must do is keep this front of mind and execute your plan accordingly. An easy next step is to book your monthly finance reviews for the next twelve months now, print out your Future Forecast and check it when planning the week ahead. Do this for a year and you should experience one of your most successful years on record. It will not take you long to realise that this is the smartest way to run a business and the way you should have been doing it all this time.

I wish you nothing but incredible success. Enjoy the journey. Make the most of those additional drawings and upgrade your lifestyle with the things that you deserve. Look after your health, stay humble, and no matter how profitable your business gets, remember: *Cash is king.*

Is your business financially fit? Get a free bespoke report on your business in five minutes to see how you are doing based on the methodologies in this book: josh-dtlqxm7w.scoreapp.com

Acknowledgements

Writing this book, *Small Business, Big Profit*, has been an incredible journey, and I would like to express my heartfelt gratitude to the individuals and organisations who have supported and inspired me along the way.

First and foremost, I would like to thank Hayley for looking after our two beautiful kids (Iris and Harvey) whenever I snuck off to get some more words written. Your belief in me and understanding of the countless hours spent writing and researching has been invaluable.

Thank you to my mum and dad who have never offered anything but support and unwavering belief as I continue to veer off the normal path and achieve things that even I did not believe possible.

I am deeply grateful to my mentor, Daniel Hill, whose guidance and expertise have been instrumental in shaping this book. Your wisdom, insights and willingness to share your knowledge have truly made a difference in the quality and impact of this work.

A special thanks for the countless clients who have supported Ultimate FD along the way, taken the plunge and shared their incredible experiences, allowing us to fundamentally shake up an outdated industry.

A huge thank you to the Ultimate FD team and all our suppliers and partners who continuously deliver World-Class results every day and free me up to do big projects like writing a book. It would not be possible without your incredible commitment and support.

Thank you to everyone who has listened to the Ultimate FD podcast, which has been a brilliant test platform for a lot of the content in this book.

Thank you to the team at Rethink Press for pushing the project forward and spending countless hours reading and suggesting edits to make everything easy to understand, and of course to my good friend and world-class editor, Zoe McMillan, who has painstakingly worked through every page and bit of text countless times.

A special thank you to my designer Shaun Gibson of Blank Design Studio for the countless hours of design support he has given me over the years.

Lastly, I would like to extend my gratitude to the readers. It is my sincerest hope that the knowledge and strategies shared within these pages help you achieve unprecedented levels of success in your own entrepreneurial journey.

Thank you all for being a part of this incredible adventure. Your contributions have been invaluable and I am truly grateful for your presence in my life.

With deepest appreciation,

Josh

The Author

 Joshua Keegan is a chartered accountant, award-winning entrepreneur, professional speaker and the founder of Ultimate FD.

Ultimate FD is a unique and proven finance business which has successfully transformed 100+ companies and received numerous accolades including Property Entrepreneur of the Year multiple times.

Having set up, scaled and sold multiple successful businesses, Joshua sits on the board of some of the UK's fastest growing companies. Joshua's belief that most entrepreneurs spend their lives building businesses that don't make money inspired his mission to change this and led to the creation of his highly regarded Ultimate FD podcast.

With a unique skillset and insight, Joshua has developed a world-class, industry-leading strategy that transforms financially related business challenges. Having effectively combined the worlds of finance and entrepreneurship, Joshua has mentored hundreds of entrepreneurs and worked with many businesses to bridge the gap between these two worlds, making finance accessible for every entrepreneur and allowing each one to make more profit and work fewer hours.

Joshua currently lives in his dream home in the Northwest of England with his partner Hayley and two children, Iris and Harvey. He balances his professional interests with a happy and loving family life and is an advocate of bringing this balance to the entrepreneurial lifestyle.

You can follow Joshua at:

f www.facebook.com/joshua.keegan

⃝ www.instagram.com/the_ultimate_fd

You can reach Joshua at:

🌐 www.ultimatefd.co.uk

Printed in Great Britain
by Amazon